Pricing Our Roads: Vision and Reality

Pricing Our Roads: Vision and Reality

STEPHEN GLAISTER
DANIEL J. GRAHAM

The Institute of Economic Affairs

First published in Great Britain in 2004 by
The Institute of Economic Affairs
2 Lord North Street
Westminster
London SW1P 3LB
in association with Profile Books Ltd

The mission of the Institute of Economic Affairs is to improve public
understanding of the fundamental institutions of a free society, with particular
reference to the role of markets in solving economic and social problems.

A CIP catalogue record for this book is available from the British Library.

ISBN 0 255 36562 4

Many IEA publications are translated into languages other than English or
are reprinted. Permission to translate or to reprint should be sought from the
Director General at the address above.

Typeset in Stone by MacGuru Ltd
info@macguru.org.uk

Printed and bound in Great Britain by Hobbs the Printers

CONTENTS

The authors	8
Foreword	9
Acknowledgements	12
Summary	13
List of maps, tables and figures	16

1 Introduction — 21
The importance of transport to the electorate — 23
The emerging transport problem: traffic congestion — 23
The need for a new policy — 27
What could road user charging offer? — 29

2 The principles behind road user charging — 31
Our general approach — 32

3 The London congestion charging scheme — 40
How congestion charging came about — 40
The outcome of congestion charging — 43

4 The data and the limitations of our analysis — 50
Data sources — 50
The maps — 54
Limitations — 55

5 Adding user charges to existing taxes 59
Environmental charges 62
Environmental charges and congestion charges 63

6 Revenue-neutral environmental and congestion charges 78

7 Fully efficient taxes and subsidies 86
Zero special taxes and subsidies 86
Zero taxes and subsidies plus environmental and
   congestion charges 88

8 How widely should charging be implemented? 94
The relationship between benefits and coverage 95
Charging thresholds 96
Geographical coverage 99

9 Road user charging in practice 105
Policy analysis 105
Technologies and enforcement 106
Privacy and human rights 107
Equity and concessions 107
Understanding the incremental costs of capacity 109
Land use planning and urban densities 110
The effect on rail finances 111
Revenue neutrality 112
European issues 113
Governance 115

10 A dream or practical policy?   118
    Congestion and environmental charges on top of today's
        fuel taxes   119
    A revenue-neutral scenario   119
    Economically efficient user charges   120
    How extensive should charging be?   122
    Location-based services: the wider vision   123
    A dream or practical policy?   125

    References   127

About the IEA   130

THE AUTHORS

Stephen Glaister

Stephen Glaister is Professor of Transport and Infrastructure at Imperial College London. He has been a member of the board of Transport for London since July 2000 and was a non-executive director of London Regional Transport from 1984 to 1993. He was a member of the steering group for the Department for Transport's National Road Pricing Feasibility Study constituted in autumn 2003. Between 1993 and spring 2001 he was an economic adviser to the Rail Regulator. He has been Specialist Adviser to the Parliamentary Select Committee on Transport, as well as an adviser to the Commission for Integrated Transport.

He has published widely on transport and also on regulation in the telecommunications, water and gas industries. In 1998 he was awarded the CBE for services to public transport

Daniel J. Graham

Dr Daniel Graham is a Senior Research Associate in the Centre for Transport Studies at Imperial College London. He received his PhD from the London School of Economics in 1996 and has subsequently worked on post-doctoral research projects on transport and urban and regional economics.

FOREWORD

IEA authors have been at the forefront of making the intellectual case for road pricing since the early 1960s. The absence of road user charges means that there are more journeys in congested areas than would take place under a system of economic pricing; journeys take place at times of day when the roads are more congested; businesses, schools and so on do not develop practices that are consistent with reducing the costs on congested transport systems; and mass transit systems have to operate in an environment in which individuals on competitor modes of transport do not pay the marginal costs of their journeys. But the problems of not pricing roads may be wider than this. It is difficult for private roads to compete with state-run roads that are free at the point of use, so private roads are virtually unknown in the UK. Also, arguably, people who live in areas where there is congestion do not pay the full economic costs of their activities, thus creating incentives for people to move from areas such as the north of England, which are less densely populated, to the south of England. Perhaps the absence of road pricing has also led to higher demand for road space in our cities, which, in turn, has led to the acquisition of land for road building which might have more valuable alternative uses.

Given the importance of transport to our economy, it is very damaging that the price system, so important for communicating information and providing incentives for people to take decisions that enhance economic welfare, is absent from the road network. The only coherent economic argument against road pricing is surely that the technology would be so expensive that the welfare benefits of road pricing would be outweighed by the costs. But the Smeed report, commissioned by the then government and published 40 years ago, concluded that, even at that time, the technology was available for an efficient road pricing system. Perhaps the real reason why road pricing has been introduced only on a limited scale – the only scheme of any significance being in central London – is because politicians fear the redistribution of income that might take place under a road pricing scheme.

This paper by Stephen Glaister and Daniel Graham may help politicians to be braver. Glaister and Graham, except in some introductory remarks, do not make the case for road pricing – it is not necessary to do so: the case is very clear and incontrovertible. Instead, in *Pricing Our Roads: Vision and Reality*, they model the practical effects of a number of different schemes, each of which, in its own way, has a sound economic basis.

Glaister and Graham use complex geographical and economic modelling to analyse the impact on traffic flows, government revenues, train and bus use, traffic speeds and costs to car drivers of different approaches to road user charging. One approach adds charges to existing taxes; another is engineered so that it is revenue-neutral; and a further approach to charging looks at an 'economically efficient' set of road user charges combined with much-reduced subsidies for buses and trains and a removal of fuel tax. It is notable that, under the economically efficient set of road user charges, with certain, quite realistic, assumptions, road users as a whole could pay approximately the same in charges as they do today under existing road taxes. Of course, some road users would pay more and others less.

Glaister and Graham's analysis should give policy-makers plenty of food for thought. There are enormous potential welfare gains from the road pricing schemes the authors examine. Yet it does seem that a charging system could be developed which ensures that motorists as a whole pay roughly the same in charges and taxes as they do at present, thus perhaps offsetting the political problems of introducing road user charging.

The authors then examine a series of practical issues, such as how widely a scheme of road user charging should be extended and whether exemptions should be made for low levels of charge. Different technical systems are considered as well as wider economic issues, such as the implications for the ownership of roads. Academics and policy-makers can learn much from the analysis in Research Monograph 59. In particular, the authors demonstrate the clear practical benefits of road user charging. They take the reader carefully through a range of practical options that will enable a better understanding of the complex issues involved in the implementation of new ways of paying for roads.

The views expressed in this Research Monograph are, as in all IEA publications, those of the author and not those of the Institute (which has no corporate view), its managing trustees, Academic Advisory Council members or senior staff.

PHILIP BOOTH

Editorial and Programme Director,
Institute of Economic Affairs,
Professor of Insurance and Risk Management,
Sir John Cass Business School, City University
June 2004

ACKNOWLEDGEMENTS

The research that forms the basis of this paper was commissioned by the Independent Transport Commission. It was funded by the Rees Jeffreys Road Fund, the Joseph Rowntree Foundation and the Esmée Fairbairn Foundation.

SUMMARY

- The provision and management of roads in the UK is one of the few remaining market-free, centrally administered sectors of the UK economy.
- Motorists pay significant amounts in tax which, in the last 25 years, has not been used to finance road provision. Taxes on motorists do not relate to the marginal costs of road use.
- Traffic congestion is a serious problem in London and other cities and vehicle use is expected to continue increasing. Rail systems already operate at capacity in those areas where roads are most congested.
- Road user charging could be adopted to ensure that motorists paid all the costs of road use, including a contribution to maintenance and depreciation, a charge reflecting the congestion costs imposed on other users, and a charge reflecting any environmental externalities.
- Road user charging has been adopted in some countries but the only notable example in the UK is the central London congestion charging scheme. This scheme, however, does not charge motorists according to the distance travelled, nor is the charge varied with differing levels of congestion. Nevertheless, the London scheme does appear to have achieved its objectives.

- Geographical and economic modelling can be used to estimate the impact of different road user charging schemes on a range of important variables such as vehicle use, train and bus use, traffic speeds and the revenue from charges. The modelling can also be used to illustrate the effects of road user charges on different types of road, in different areas and at different times of day.

- The addition of economic road user charges to existing taxes on petrol and vehicle ownership might yield revenues to the Treasury of about £10 billion – although the revenue estimate is sensitive to the assumptions made. User charges would also lead to substantial welfare benefits, increases in traffic speeds, and a reduction in road use of about 9 per cent. Most of the benefits of increased speed would be concentrated in particular areas. There would, of course, be substantial extra costs for motorists from this policy.

- If reductions were made to existing taxes on motorists, or if the charging structure were designed to alleviate some of the extra burden of charges on road users by offering them rebates, there could be even greater benefits from user charges. There is a smaller overall reduction in traffic and a smaller increase in traffic speeds from such a policy as the cost of motoring does not necessarily increase. Traffic would increase in non-congested areas and decrease in congested areas. This efficient redistribution of road use towards less congested areas might be even more marked if some of the assumptions, necessary for the modelling exercise, were relaxed.

- In developing a system of road user charges, consideration has to be given to how widely it should be implemented.

The marginal benefits of collecting low charges in non-congested areas should be compared with the marginal costs of collection: this would, in turn, depend on the technology used. Most of the benefits of user charging arise in relatively small areas of the country at particular times of day.

- If road user charging were implemented, it could open up discussion on a range of other policy issues regarding the ownership, governance and management of the road system: competition would be possible between different providers of roads; the information to enable investment decisions to be taken would be much improved; there may be concern about government agencies controlling the whole network and thereby collecting the information about where individual motorists travel; and the technology and infrastructure used for user charging may have a range of other applications.

MAPS, TABLES AND FIGURES

Maps

1 22% traffic growth – effects on road speeds   67
2 22% traffic growth – effects on road traffic   68
3 Environmental charges and congestion charges –
   effects on road speeds   69
4 Environmental charges and congestion charges –
   effects on road traffic   70
5 Environmental charges and congestion charges, revenue-
   neutral tax adjustment – effects on road speeds   71
6 Environmental charges and congestion charges, revenue-
   neutral tax adjustment – effects on road traffic   72
7 Zero taxes and subsidies – speed changes   73
8 Zero taxes and subsidies – traffic changes   74
9 Zero fuel duty, economic environmental charges and
   congestion charges, low environmental costs –
   effects on road speeds   75
10 Zero fuel duty, environmental charges and congestion
   charges, low environmental costs – effects on road traffic   76

Tables

1 The consequences of 22% traffic demand growth 27
2 Forecast scheme revenues and costs for financial year
2003/04 48
3 Preliminary estimates of costs and benefits of the central
London congestion charging scheme 48
4 Road costs, Great Britain, 1998 prices and values 53
5 The result of adding charges to existing taxes 60
6 Economic evaluation: adding charges to existing taxes 61
7 Results of revenue-neutral environmental and
congestion charges 79
8 Economic evaluation: revenue-neutral environmental
and congestion charges 80
9 Fully efficient taxes and subsidies 87
10 Economic evaluation: fully efficient taxes and subsidies 89
11 Revenues and charges by road type: area types 1–6 102
12 Revenues and charges by road type: area types 1–8 102
13 Revenues and charges by road type: all area types 103

Figures

1 The economics of road user charging 34
2 Traffic entering the charging zone during charging hours
on a representative selection of major entry points 44
3 Congestion levels in the charging zone during
charging hours 45
4 Current fuel tax rates, environmental charges and
congestion charges (low environmental costs) 64
5 Environmental charges and congestion charges; revenue-
neutral tax adjustment (low environment costs) 82

6   The effects of waiving low rates of charge   97
7   Rates of charge by region   98
8   The effects of extending charging from central London
    to less urbanised areas   100

Pricing Our Roads: Vision and Reality

1 INTRODUCTION

The provision of roads in the UK, and the management of their use, is one of the few remaining market-free, centrally administered sectors of the UK economy. There are no explicit charges for the use of the system. Expenditure on maintenance and new capacity is ultimately controlled by Whitehall.

Yet when a user purchases fuel, well over half the price at the pump is accounted for by taxation. This could be argued to be a charge but nobody thinks in those terms. Unlike in a properly functioning market the price of fuel to the user bears no relation to the direct costs of service, costs imposed on others, the benefits they enjoy or their willingness to pay for better service. Nor does the total tax revenue bear any relation to public expenditure on transport: Coates (1999) notes that in 1975 road taxation totalled £12.8 billion and spending on local roads, local public transport and national roads totalled £11.5 billion (figures in 1998 prices). By 1997/98 tax had risen to over £31 billion and spending had fallen to under £6 billion. So what was once a rough balance has changed to a considerable imbalance. This trend has continued. It is not clear that many people are aware of this, or how it has occurred. Traffic has grown relentlessly as real incomes and economic activity have increased, and there has been a steady increase in the rate of fuel duty. Consequently the yield from fuel duty has grown to be a very important source of Exchequer revenues – largely sumptuary taxation.

In the absence of any market mechanism the UK government has, since the 1960s, been a world leader in developing cost–benefit-based methods for the scientific appraisal of investments in road schemes. This was evidenced by the report of the Independent Advisory Committee on Trunk Road Assessment (1976). Sadly, these techniques have been overwhelmed by the inevitable administrative and political pressures of the public spending decision-making process. Allocation of public expenditure to the transport sector and within the sector bears less and less relation to any objective justification. This has become particularly marked since the turn of the century with the apparently uncontrollable drift of funding in favour of the railways (see Glaister, 2002).

The outcome of a lack of market signals and centralised planning has been what one would expect: under-provision in some places with the limited capacity being rationed by queuing in the form of traffic congestion; over-provision in other places with expensive infrastructure offering excessive capacity of little economic value; commerce and the general public paying a great deal for their use of the roads but with no mechanism through which they might express their preferences for paying more (or less) for better (or worse) standards of service.

The constructive use of road user charging could introduce a valuable new dimension to transport policy. It could be used to simultaneously contain traffic growth at times and places where congestion is a problem, while ameliorating environmental damage and reducing the pressure to increase road capacity. In other words it could both achieve more efficient use of the existing transport infrastructures and offer the right signals about when, where and to what extent it would be worthwhile investing in new capacity.

The importance of transport to the electorate

Transport matters to the public, and we spend far more on it than we used to. The annual Family Expenditure Survey reveals that in 1962 households allocated about 9 per cent of their expenditure to transport and 33 per cent to food, alcohol and tobacco. Now transport, at 15 per cent, is second only to expenditure on housing and utilities at 18 per cent, while food, alcohol and tobacco account only for 13 per cent. Most of this household transport spending is on owning and running private vehicles. While car ownership is not universal it is far more common than it used to be: car availability (including as passengers and the use of taxis) has spread much farther among the young, the older population and poorer households than is commonly realised. This has been the result of increasing real incomes, demographic changes, generally falling real costs of motoring and spectacular improvements in the quality of the vehicles that can be purchased for a modest sum.

Meanwhile public transport has become much less relevant, with the exception of some special markets such as commuter routes to London. Only 6 per cent of UK passenger kilometres travelled are by rail, and the Strategic Rail Authority notes that more than half the population uses a train less than once a year (SRA, 2003). Rail accounts for 5 per cent, bus accounts for 6 per cent and car for 85 per cent of all passenger kilometres (excluding walking). Rail now carries 8 per cent of freight tonne kilometres.

The emerging transport problem: traffic congestion

The Labour government's Transport White Paper (DETR, 2000a) generally failed to come to grips with these realities, but since then the UK government has slowly begun to respond to the electoral implications of these rapid and fundamental changes. The government's response to the fuel protests of autumn 2000 was an early example. Tax on road fuels had been increasing at 5 per cent per year above inflation in the latter years of the Conservative government, and the 1997 Labour government increased this to 6 per cent. The rationale offered by Labour was that traffic growth had to be stopped and that road users should be given stronger incentives to reduce damaging emissions. This policy succeeded in meeting its objectives. It also raised a great deal of tax revenue, though neither government declared that as an explicit objective. But the Labour government quickly abandoned the policy in late 2000 when a rapid rise in the world price of oil compounded the tax rate increases and precipitated the fuel protests.

Traffic growth in Britain is placing an increasingly heavy burden on our road infrastructure capacity. If present policies are maintained England could have 25 per cent more traffic by 2010 than it did in 2000 (DETR, 2000b; DfT, 2003). Relentlessly worsening traffic congestion reminds many voters on a daily basis that there is a transport problem. The welcome announcement in December 2002 (DfT, 2002) of a carefully targeted and modest increase in road building may have been a response to this. Even more welcome was the recognition by the Secretary of State for Transport in July 2003 (DfT, 2003) that under current policies things will inevitably continue to deteriorate and that road user charging should be seriously investigated as one of the practical ways of dealing with the problem.

Some of the factors causing the anticipated traffic growth are: the hoped-for increase in real incomes; rapid improvement in the fuel efficiency of cars; and the current policy of allowing the pump prices of fuel to fall in real terms as crude oil prices fall in real terms. Meanwhile, the presently planned increases in road capacity will not match this growth in demand – and a decision to greatly expand road building, were it to be made, could not make much difference for many years because of the time it takes to deliver new road projects. Consequently congestion looks set to get worse in many locations.

To illustrate, assume there was no change in real taxes or charges but a 22 per cent increase in the underlying demand for all modes of transport. This could result from ten years' compound growth in real incomes at 2 per cent per annum and is just short of the government's own prediction of 25 per cent more traffic by the year 2010 (DETR, 2000b). Also assume that there were no changes in road capacity above that existing in 2000. Maps 1 and 2 (on pages 67 and 68) indicate the effect on road speed and road traffic.

Map 1 indicates the predicted effects on average speeds in England. The method we have used to construct these maps is explained below. For all the maps in this document we have adopted the convention that blue means that things have got better compared with today's base and red means they have got worse. 'Better' means higher speeds or less traffic and 'worse' means lower speeds or more traffic. Clearly, more traffic is not necessarily bad from an economic perspective – 'worse' simply means that traffic has increased or slowed down, indicating worsening driving conditions for a given road capacity.

The areas of stress show up in red. They are London and the motorway corridors into London, the West Midlands conurbation and some other urban centres, including Tyneside. There is an important medium stress band stretching from Manchester to Leeds and Bradford. Otherwise there is little speed reduction due to increased congestion in the North, South-west and East Anglian regions, where there is spare capacity outside the large towns. This map of stresses bears a resemblance to the map published in 1998 by the then DETR (2000a). These changes are averages across day and night and across the week, so they disguise the fact that at peak times within the week the speed reduction would be considerably worse than the average.

Map 2 shows the corresponding road traffic increases. Because speeds have reduced so much in London, time costs of travel have increased and the traffic growth is held to less than 5 per cent. At any given level of money cost and time cost the demand has grown by 22 per cent, but higher time costs due to traffic congestion then 'choke off' part of the underlying growth in traffic demand. Although Map 2 indicates that traffic growth is less in London and the South-east than in other areas, this is only because the effect of an increase in traffic on speed is so great in already congested areas that the decrease in speed and increase in traffic generated in turn chokes off some of that increase in traffic. Even after allowing for that effect, the impact on speeds is still much greater in the areas indicated in red in Map 1.

The two maps exhibit the weight of activity in London and the South-east regions and clear North–South and East–West divides – a feature that is characteristic of many of our results.

The overall effect on the national transport systems is shown in the second line of Table 1. Nationally there is a 20 per cent increase in road traffic: not the full 22 per cent because of the deterrent effect of increasing congestion and reduced speeds. There is a 24 per cent increase in rail patronage. The financial position of the railways improves by £0.77 billion per annum (neglecting any operating or capital costs involved). The Exchequer receives £4.2 billion per annum in additional fuel tax revenues at current rates.

Table 1 **The consequences of 22% traffic demand growth**

	Traffic	All passenger km	Car km	Commercial vehicle km
	—— Ratio of flow to the current value[1] ——			
Current (2003)	1	1	1	1
22% demand growth	1.20	1.20	1.19	1.20

	Bus passenger km	Rail passenger km	Car cost £ per km	Bus subsidy	Rail subsidy
	— Ratio of flow to the current value[1] —			£m p.a.	£m p.a.
Current (2003)	1	1	0.104	1,408	1,597
22% demand growth	1.20	1.24	0.104	1,425	828

1 For example, a ratio of 1.2 would normally be interpreted as a 20 per cent increase and a ratio of 0.94 as a 6 per cent reduction.

There is an increase in environmental damage costs of £1.2 billion per annum.

The need for a new policy

The future growth scenario just described is a significant over-simplification of the vision implied by policy statements by the Secretary of State in December 2002. Our interpretation of these policy statements is as follows:

- A 50 per cent increase in passenger rail traffic.
- A 20 per cent increase in bus traffic in London and a 10 per cent increase outside London.
- A 20 per cent improvement in the average fuel efficiency of cars and a 13 per cent improvement in the average fuel efficiency of commercial vehicles.

- Fuel price to the user to fall from the value we have used of
  £0.80 per litre to, say, £0.70 per litre (in today's prices).
- Values of time would increase as real incomes increase,
  perhaps by 20 per cent or so.

Taken together these assumptions would imply substantially more increased demand for road traffic growth than the 22 per cent used in our illustration. For instance, the combined effect of improving fuel efficiency and a fall in the real fuel price would reduce the real cost of fuel per vehicle kilometre by over 30 per cent. This set of assumptions might lead to an average 25 per cent increase in road traffic by 2010 *after* accounting for the deterrent effect of worsening traffic delays.

The House of Commons Transport Committee (2003) concluded that:

> Improvements in technology and public transport alone
> will not solve our congestion and pollution problems. The
> only effective way of achieving a sustained cut in congestion
> appears to be to introduce some road user charging on
> our busiest roads during peak periods. Introducing inter-
> urban charging will be a difficult decision to take, and
> the assumption has been that it would be unpopular. But
> the alternative is increasing congestion and pollution, a
> proposition which we find unacceptable and potentially
> more unpopular.

The Select Committee also notes that even if there were the political will to develop sufficient capacity to meet the forecast demands for travel by road, bus and rail, the cost implications would be unaffordable in terms of the current public spending environment.

While we cannot be precise in this study about the level of charges and revenues that might be appropriate by 2010, it is plain that the pressure to introduce some radical new policy such as general road user charging will become much stronger by then than it is today.

What could road user charging offer?

This is a study of what, in principle, road user charges across the whole of England might have to offer if they reflected properly the costs that road users impose on one another and on third parties. We start from the proposition that to date 'prices' have been set on the basis of historical precedent or political expediency and their potential use as a tool of efficient transport management has not been given sufficient attention.

While people generally use some phrase such as 'congestion charging' (and that is appropriate for the London scheme), our study concerns 'road user charging' because it also accounts for other costs in addition to congestion, such as road maintenance, additional accident costs and environmental costs such as noise, air pollution and greenhouse gas emissions.

We present results that allow for a comparison of the current structure of transport taxes and charges with that implied by several policy scenarios.

Having presented these alternatives we discuss a number of the issues of political economy that would have to be resolved by any government seeking to introduce a practical policy of national road user charging. We do not seek to raise difficulties in order to be negative or to denigrate the policy. On the contrary, we can see little alternative to user charging in some form sooner or later, and the sooner it can be introduced the more good it can do. We think the difficulties are real, are less tractable than some people appear to believe, and have to be identified and dealt with.

2 THE PRINCIPLES BEHIND ROAD USER CHARGING

The economic principles underlying road user charging are long established. In an essay written just after World War II, Professor Milton Friedman outlined a proposal involving putting radioactive material into road markings and recording the use a vehicle had made of the roads by vehicle-mounted Geiger counters: a nice example of the right economic principles being proposed for implementation through impractical technology.

The theory was completely specified in Sir Alan Walters' (1961) seminal article 'The theory and measurement of private and social costs of highway congestion'. An official UK committee under the chairmanship of Ruben Smeed (1964) thought road pricing both timely and technologically practicable. Colin Buchanan (1963) correctly and far-sightedly diagnosed the traffic growth problem in his influential *Traffic in Towns*, but he did not embrace pricing as a possible solution. In passing he did mention 'a system of pricing the use of road space' as one of four options, but then said no more about it. His masterly analysis of what would have to be done if traffic growth were not tamed caused much alarm. It is a shame that in the debate that followed his publication the use of pricing as a way of achieving the reduction of traffic growth was not given any attention. It was the drastic implications for the urban landscape of attempting to accommodate traffic growth which grabbed the attention of the press.

Since then several authors have articulated the case for road user charging (for example, Hibbs and Roth, 1992; Hibbs, 1993; Roth 1995). There was an experimental electronic scheme in Hong Kong and a long-standing, successful paper-based scheme in Singapore (now converted to an electronic system). Small-scale bridge and individual highway tolling systems have worked without difficulty, and several Scandinavian towns are operating charges for crossing a town boundary, often as a revenue-raising rather than as a congestion-reducing measure. Large-scale paper-based systems were seriously proposed for London on two occasions, and one would have been implemented had the relevant motion at the Greater London Council not been lost by a single vote (see Greater London Council, 1974).

Our general approach

We have used a simple and conventional approach to model the consequences of the various road user charging policies. The 'generalised' cost to a user of a specific mode, in a particular place at a particular time of day, is a measure of the money value of the total of all the costs faced per person kilometre (for example, the money cost or fare, plus the cost of in-vehicle time, plus the cost of waiting time, plus taxation, plus any other relevant costs). Our approach assumes that the demand for any one mode is dependent on the generalised cost of using that mode and on the generalised cost of using all other modes.[1] This represents the propensity to

---

1   A detailed specification of the methodology underpinning our model can be found in Glaister and Graham (2003a; 2003b) and Graham and Glaister (2003). The formulation used for demand is the semi-logarithmic form which has the property that own-price elasticities are directly proportional to own prices.

switch between modes in response to changes in relative money charges or congestion.

Figure 1 provides a graphical illustration. The vertical axis represents the generalised cost per passenger or vehicle kilometre and the horizontal axis represents the flow of passenger kilometres per hour. The marginal private cost and marginal social cost lines are illustrated, intersecting the demand curve. These are, respectively, the cost borne by a particular individual of making an extra one-kilometre trip and the cost to all individuals (including social costs borne by others) of one particular individual making an extra one-kilometre trip. The vertical distance between the lines represents (for any given flow) the difference between the costs borne by the individual user and costs imposed on everybody else. These will be time-delay costs from extra congestion and various other external costs such as accident risk, noise and pollution, all of which must be represented in money terms.

For example, at the flow $x°_i$ the cost in terms of the value of time and money spent of an individual travelling one additional kilometre might be £0.10 (point A). But the act of travelling that extra kilometre will cause a little extra pollution cost to others, slow down all the existing traffic somewhat and cause wear and tear on a road. So the total cost to society of the extra trip might be the £0.10 plus £0.03: leading to a marginal social cost of £0.13 (point D).

The demand relationship shown in the figure represents the way the demand might respond to changes in generalised cost. We establish an initial equilibrium at point A where demand (x^o_i) is related to a level of generalised cost assuming the user pays the

---

Therefore price elasticities are not constant: as a price rises people become more responsive to changes in the cost of using the mode.

Figure 1   **The economics of road user charging**

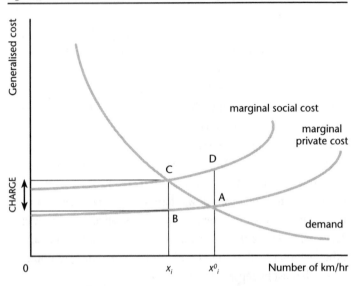

private marginal cost of making a trip. The efficient generalised cost and flow, given a free hand to adjust taxes and prices, is given by the point where the benefit of an extra kilometre is just in balance with the marginal social costs: point C, with the reduced demand, x_i. This could be achieved by imposing a unit charge represented by the distance between B and C. Therefore, put simply, our aim is to estimate the point C.

We take the situation in 2000 as a base set of flows of vehicles and people. We establish this as an equilibrium, in which traffic flows, demands, speeds and generalised costs are mutually consistent. That is, equilibrium speeds imply a set of generalised costs which imply a set of demands for the use of the network which implies a level of traffic which implies the equilibrium speeds. We then estimate new equilibria following changes in generalised costs brought about by the imposition of new charging regimes.

This approach recognises three fundamental linkages. First, varying prices will change volumes which, in turn, will lead to variations in important dimensions of quality, such as speed, as congestion changes. Second, varying prices and times will affect the mode of travel. Third, varying prices, taxes and subsidies will change the burden on the public purse and may change the funding available for new infrastructure both from public sources and from privately funded investment. Differing pricing regimes will create changes in patterns of demand, and consequently changes in the case for investment in infrastructure.

The steps for computing the movement from point A to point C are as follows:

1 Establish a base equilibrium in which speeds, traffic flows, demands and generalised costs are mutually consistent.
2 Set up the appropriate responses of demand to price (the demand elasticities) and the relationships between changes in traffic flow and changes in speeds (the speed/flow relationships).
3 Make a change to a policy variable such as a public transport fare, a tax on fuel or a road user charge per vehicle kilometre.
4 Calculate a new equilibrium with a new mutually consistent set of speeds, generalised costs and demands.

This last stage involves an iterative process of calculation because of the many interdependencies. An example is shown in the box overleaf.

Suppose that in the initial situation, as represented by point A in Figure 1 (on page 34), the uncharged road is carrying 100 vehicle kilometres per hour, and the time and money costs to the vehicle users amount to £0.10 per vehicle kilometre. Then, to reflect external costs, an additional charge of £0.03 per vehicle kilometre is imposed. This is represented by point D.

The demand relationship indicates that traffic must fall: by construction the 'last' vehicle on to the road was willing to pay a maximum of £0.10, so some traffic will be deterred by the new charge bringing the total cost to the user to £0.13. This would take us to a point to the left of points C and D, say to a traffic flow of 90.

But there is now less traffic and congestion will be less severe, so the £0.03 is now too high a charge to reflect the external costs imposed by each user on all the others. So the user charge should be reduced from £0.03 to, say, £0.025.

Then traffic will increase, perhaps to a point to the right of points C and D, say to 96.

And so the process continues until it converges to point C, where traffic is, say, 95.

At this point a new equilibrium is established in which the 'last' vehicle on to the road is just willing to pay its own costs and the user charge and that user charge just balances the costs the 'last' vehicle (and any other vehicle) imposes on the totality of all other vehicles. Each vehicle is paying the full 'marginal social cost' of its decision to use the road.

Establishing the equilibrium set of charges corresponding to point C in Figure 1 also yields estimates of the revised volumes of travel and hence the changes to tax revenues and public transport costs, revenues and subsidies. Thus an estimate is produced of the overall net effect on the public finances.

At the new equilibrium traffic level, congestion and pollution have all fallen and the road user charge has generated revenue. Road users generally are made worse off because they are either paying more or they have been deterred from travelling. But it can be demonstrated that, in principle, there is more than enough revenue to compensate them so that everyone can end up better off. This is a reflection of the fact that the facility is being more efficiently used so that the overall economic value of the system is increased.

This is one reason for the crucial importance of the issue of what happens to the revenues from road user charging. If, as may well be the case in practice, the revenues are not used to compensate those paying the charge in some way, then those groups will be disadvantaged. That is why the decision to legislate to ensure that London congestion charging proceeds must be applied to transport purposes in London was crucial to securing public support – at least the net revenues must remain in the transport sector and in the relevant geographical area. This is perhaps not ideal as it may encourage over-investment in public transport projects that do not produce an adequate economic return. Allowing local authorities (including the GLA) to reduce the council tax or non-domestic property taxes using road charging revenues would be an alternative way of enabling revenues to be returned to local people, although this creates problems because local authority boundaries are not necessarily coincident with charging zones. At a national level, of course, charges can be returned by reducing vehicle excise duty (see below). This desire to use net revenues to compensate the losers in the transition from one method of levying taxes for road use to another raises the issue of the costs of charge collection and enforcement. If they are too high there will not be enough net revenue left to compensate the losers, even in principle. Indeed the economic value created through efficient pricing could be more than consumed by the scheme's administration.

This description is oversimplified because in reality, and in our model, charged roads will be used by individuals with a range of values of time saving. When charges are introduced, those with the higher values will be more inclined to stay on the road, pay the charge and enjoy the benefit of higher speed. Therefore the scarce and valuable resource, road space, is reallocated to those who gain the greater value from using it. This is a further source of economic efficiency. Even without compensation, road users as a group may gain overall. There might also be economic welfare benefits that go beyond the benefits arising purely in the transport sector. For example, the overall costs of living in a congested area (say, the South-east) will be more closely matched by the costs the individuals that live there pay. Individuals can take economically more efficient decisions about where they live, where they locate their businesses, and so on.

Bus users will also benefit from higher speeds and greater reliability, and bus operating companies will enjoy reduced operating costs. This will ultimately be reflected in lower demands for subsidy from the taxpayer.

It is apparent that any particular proposal for levying charges and disbursing the revenues may have significant implications for the distribution of welfare among road users of differing incomes and between road users and others. In Chapters 5 to 8 we examine the impact of various different charging schemes. Some of these schemes involve levying close to what might be regarded as economically efficient prices. Others use slightly different criteria for charging for particular economic, political and practical reasons discussed below.

3 THE LONDON CONGESTION CHARGING SCHEME

The prospects for more extensive use of road user charging have been transformed by the experience with the London congestion charging scheme introduced by the executive Mayor of London, Ken Livingstone, in February 2003. Whether or not this scheme is ultimately judged to have been a success, it has already achieved a most important change. It has demonstrated to the general public and to politicians that charging for the use of roads is a practical policy that can make a real difference to behaviour and to congestion levels. It can make a real improvement to the level of service enjoyed by remaining road users, in particular bus and taxi users, and by pedestrians.

How congestion charging came about

The London congestion charging scheme would have been very much less likely to have come to fruition had it not been for the coincidence of several factors. In 1986 Mrs Thatcher's Conservative government abolished the local authority, the Greater London Council, and took much of the administration of London back into Whitehall, although some powers – notably concerning education – were passed to the thirty-three London boroughs (where they remain). The leader of the GLC at the time was Ken Livingstone, a radical Labour Party member.

When the government changed in 1997, Labour had made commitments to devolution in general and in particular to the creation of a new Greater London Authority (GLA). There was to be a directly elected assembly and a directly elected, executive mayor: a major innovation in UK local authority governance. It was recognised at the outset that transport would be one of the most important areas of responsibility for the GLA.

The legislation was controversial and complicated. It took until 2000 to be completed as the Greater London Act 2000. The legislation enables a mayor to introduce a congestion charging scheme or a workplace parking charging scheme, the revenues from which would be mandated for transport purposes in the Greater London area. The decision to insist on the 'hypothecation' of the net revenues in this manner was highly unusual in UK governance. It was the outcome of a hard-fought battle during which the Treasury was persuaded that it was a necessary condition for the political acceptability of a scheme.

With commendable foresight, two years before completion of the legislation, the Government Office for London (the Whitehall department with special responsibility for London matters) set up a study group of civil servants and outside experts to propose outline designs to be offered to an incoming mayor should he or she wish to introduce a charging scheme. At that stage it was not known who the candidates for mayor might be.

The group duly researched the matter and published a report, 'Road Charging Options for London' (RoCOL, Government Office for London, 2000), which explained its recommended schemes. In the event, candidates for mayor representing the established political parties showed little interest in such a policy. In particular the Labour government and the official Labour Party candidate were lukewarm about it in spite of having created the necessary powers. Ken Livingstone had wanted to stand as the official Labour Party candidate in the hope and expectation of being seen to reverse the Conservatives' abolition of the GLC in 1986. But he was rejected as candidate and excluded from the Labour Party so he stood as an independent. He saw value in a radical innovation and perceived sufficiently strong electoral support to take the risk of including a manifesto commitment to introduce one of RoCOL's recommended congestion charging schemes. As with all the candidates, improving public transport was an important part of his offering, and he was able to present congestion charging in the context of a coherent overall transport package. Livingstone was always a strong candidate, not least because he had been the leader of the GLC at the time it had been abolished, an action that had caused resentment among the London electorate irrespective of political persuasion.

Once elected Livingstone was able quickly to include the scheme in the draft of his statutory Transport Strategy and to move to statutory public consultation on the detail. He had a clear electoral mandate for the scheme, and it was sufficiently well worked out to withstand the inevitable attempts to stop it through judicial review. Crucially, the chosen scheme had been designed to ensure that it could be implemented well within a mayor's first four-year term of office, leaving time for it to settle down before the next election in June 2004. The need to implement the scheme quickly and to minimise the technological, administrative and political risks – factors that RoCOL had identified as likely to be crucial – explains the somewhat unadventurous and expensive design that was selected. Livingstone was re-admitted to the Labour Party and was re-elected in June 2004. The principal opposition candidate had said he would withdraw congestion charging.

In short, the factors enabling successful implementation were: time spent on careful preliminary research into a specific, practical and reliable scheme design; a major discontinuity in governance arrangements; and a radical, independent politician with sufficient personal support to win the election, willing to take risks.

The outcome of congestion charging

Figures 2 and 3 illustrate the London congestion charging scheme's effect. Transport for London's (2003: para. 1.11) summary of the scheme after six months of operation includes the following:

- Drivers in the charging zone are spending less time in traffic queues, with time spent either stationary or travelling at below 10 kilometres per hour now reduced by about a quarter.
- Journey times to, from and across the charging zone have decreased by an average of 14 per cent. Journey time reliability has improved by an average of 30 per cent.
- Traffic management arrangements have successfully accommodated traffic diverting to the boundary route around the congestion charging zone.
- About 60,000 fewer cars per day now come into the charging zone.
- Transport for London estimate that 20 to 30 per cent of these reduced car movements have diverted around the zone; that 50 to 60 per cent represent transfers to public transport; and that 15 to 25 per cent represent switching to car share, motorcycle or pedal cycle, or other adaptations such as

PRICING OUR ROADS: VISION AND REALITY

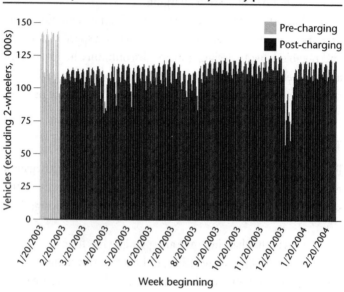

Figure 2 **Traffic entering the charging zone during charging hours on a representative selection of major entry points**

travelling outside charging hours or making fewer trips to the charging zone.

- Fears of increased parking around suburban rail stations have not materialised.

- Early data on accidents within the congestion charging zone suggest that these are at least continuing to fall broadly in line with pre-charging trends, although a full evaluation of the road safety effects will take several years.

- Congestion charging is expected to generate £68 million this financial year (2003/04) for spending on transport improvements, and £80 million to £100 million in future years.

Figure 3   Congestion levels in the charging zone during charging hours

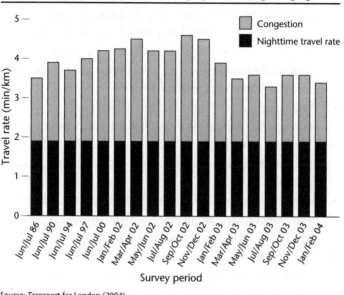

Source: Transport for London (2004)

After the first year of operation, Transport for London (2004: p. 1) further concluded that:

- Driver responses to charging remain settled: traffic data, payments data and other survey information all continue to point to new settled patterns of travel.
- Traffic delays inside the charging zone average 30 per cent lower than before charging was introduced.
- Provisional estimates of year-on-year changes in traffic levels during charging hours show a reduction of 15 per cent in traffic circulating within the zone, and a reduction of 18 per

cent in traffic entering the zone during charging hours.

- There remains no evidence of any significant adverse traffic impacts from the scheme outside the zone. Traffic management arrangements continue to successfully accommodate traffic diverting on to the boundary route, and more widely in inner London.

- Public transport continues to cope well with ex-car users: additional bus capacity is accommodating extra passengers travelling to the zone, both as a result of charging and as part of the wider trend towards increased bus travel throughout London.

- Buses continue to demonstrate significant gains in reliability in and around the charging zone, with up to a 60 per cent reduction in disruption caused by traffic delays.

- Surveys of over 700 businesses inside and immediately outside the charging zone have shown that wider economic and other factors were reported most frequently as influences on recent business performance; congestion charging constituted only 12 per cent of the reported influences.

- When asked whether they support congestion charging as long as there is continued investment in public transport, around 60 per cent of the surveyed businesses said they did and only around 20 per cent said they did not.

- Further analysis of economic trends and other data are confirming the key influence that 'external' factors had on the central London retail economy during the first half of 2003, and that the direct congestion charging effects on retail performance are small.

- The improvements in congestion, public transport and amenity are being recognised by businesses and Londoners.

- A phased programme of improvements to the enforcement service is also being introduced. In line with this the number of Penalty Charge Notices (PCNs) issued has increased with an average of some 165,000 per month, while representations made in response to PCNs have fallen from 64 per cent in the early weeks of the scheme to a recent level of about 22 per cent. This indicates both increased familiarity with the scheme and improvements in its operational systems.

One of the most controversial aspects of the scheme remains the effect it may have had on the retail trade within the congestion charging zone and on business more generally. Transport for London (2004) discusses this issue at length, noting that one has to interpret the evidence with considerable care because of the coincidence of several unrelated but influential events, such as the closure of the Central Line for a period of months and a slump in national and international tourism. It will be some time before the effects – good and bad – on business can be reliably identified (see also Bell et al., 2004). One of many controversial issues here is the extent to which one should be concerned only with the impact on the businesses within the charging zone, or whether the relevant area is the whole of the urban area.

Table 2 summarises the revenues and costs forecast for the first year of operation. Forecast net revenue for 2004/05 onwards is £80–£100 million per year, and costs are expected to fall in subsequent years. It is notable that in the first year the costs are of the order of two-thirds of the gross revenues. This is a reflection of the extremely expensive nature of the particular technological and administrative systems chosen, for reasons already noted.

Table 3 gives a preliminary economic appraisal of the London

Table 2 **Forecast scheme revenues and costs for financial year 2003/04 (£ million)**

Revenues	
Residents (at 50p per day)	2
Vehicles (at £5 per day)	102
Fleet vehicles (at £5.50 per day)	11
Total congestion charge payment	**115**
Penalty Charge Payments	50
Total gross revenue	**165**
Costs	
Operating costs 2003/04 (reduces in subsequent years)	97
Net revenues	**68**

Source: Transport for London (2003), para. 4.9

Table 3 **Preliminary estimates of costs and benefits of the central London congestion charging scheme (£ million per year, rounded)**

Annual costs	
TfL administrative and other costs	5
Scheme operation	90
Additional bus costs	20
Charge-payer compliance costs	15
Total	**130**
Annual benefits	
Time savings to car and taxi occupants, business use	75
Time savings to car and taxi occupants, private use	40
Time savings to commercial vehicle occupants	20
Time savings to bus passengers	20
Reliability benefits to car, taxi and commercial vehicle occupants	10
Reliability benefits to bus passengers	10
Vehicle fuel and operating savings	10
Accident savings	15
Disbenefit to car occupants transferring to public transport, etc.	−20
Total	**180**

Source: Transport for London (2003), para. 5.12

scheme. Despite the high costs there is an estimated excess of economic benefit – mainly from time savings – over the costs. It is clear, however, that if congestion charging is to be worthwhile in revenue and economic benefit terms in a less congested city than central London, then ways must be found to reduce the costs.

4 THE DATA AND THE LIMITATIONS OF OUR ANALYSIS

In order to establish our representation of the initial 'base' situation, data are required on travel demands, values of time, vehicle operating costs, traffic speeds, external costs, and travel demand elasticities. In this chapter we describe the sources of our data and then describe the way in which the data were used to produce the maps that present the results visually. This description is a basic overview of the models and approaches used and of our data sources. A full presentation of the technicalities of the models and data sources is in the references contained within this chapter. The approach used involves complex geographical and economic modelling. It is not necessary to understand the models in detail in order to understand the results presented in the chapters following this one. Full verification of the results, however, would, of course, require a detailed knowledge and application of the models used to predict transport usage, revenues, costs and so on.

Data sources

Road traffic demand data

Detailed road traffic flow data were provided by the UK Department for Transport (DfT). These data relate to England for the year 2000 and were used to create a 'base' set of figures to represent the situation in 2000. The data represent flows of private cars, buses, light goods vehicles, heavy goods vehicles and articulated goods vehicles. The data for private cars are further disaggregated by six journey purposes.

England is divided into the nine English Government Office Regions and the data are further divided by type of road, a variety of different urban and rural area types and nineteen different times of the week. This yields 4,480 categories, and for each of these there is a 'busy' and a 'not busy' direction giving a total of 8,960 'cases'.

Public transport demand data

Public transport demand data were derived from published sources, principally *Transport Statistics, Great Britain* (DTLR, 2001a) and *Regional Transport Statistics* (DTLR, 2001b). We derived estimates for bus and rail passenger kilometres by region and for average bus and rail fares paid. While bus fares varied by region, rail fares did not because we could not secure satisfactory rail receipts data by region. A national average was used for rail.

Values of time

Values of time in 1998 prices were taken from the DfT's *Transport Economics Note* (DETR, 2001) and adjusted to allow for inflation and real income growth between 1998 and 2003 (ibid.: Table 2/7).

Vehicle operating costs

The DfT's *Transport Economics Note* provides vehicle operating cost formulae. Fuel efficiency gains between 1998 and 2003 were applied (see DETR, 2001: Table 3/4). Fuel was assumed to be priced at £0.80 per litre for cars and commercial vehicles and at £0.34 per litre for public service vehicles, after rebate of fuel duty. We assumed that bus average loads would stay constant so that the total capacity would be adjusted in step with the volume of patronage; we also assumed that bus costs varied in direct proportion with patronage. For rail we were unable to determine a defensible assumption on how rail costs might vary with rail traffic. We therefore assumed that train services and hence train costs would be unchanged throughout, changes in patronage being accommodated by changes in average train loadings. In cases where rail demand falls this may be realistic. In cases where it rises then it is unrealistic because the railway is already at or near full capacity in many cases (for instance, in the London peak commuter market).

Traffic speeds and speed/flow relationships

For each road type and area type in our road traffic data we had information that allowed us to estimate speeds. Speed/flow relationships are crucial to the computation of the costs of congestion because they represent the way in which speeds reduce as traffic increases. The ones we used were suggested by the DfT.

Transport cost data

For the private and social costs of vehicle trips we used the figures given in the study of road and rail transport costs in Britain by Sansom et al. (2001). They provide estimates of the external costs of road and rail travel specifying costs related to infrastructure operation, external accident, air pollution, noise and climatic

Table 4 **Road costs (pence per vehicle km), Great Britain, 1998 prices and values**

Cost category	Low	High
Infrastructure operating costs and depreciation	0.42	0.54
External accident costs	0.82	1.40
Air pollution	0.34	1.70
Noise	0.02	0.05
Climate change	0.15	0.62

Source: Sansom et al. (2001)

change. Some of the values we used are shown in Table 4. Separate estimates are presented for different vehicle types, area types and infrastructure types. We estimated the marginal social costs of congestion ourselves, computing them numerically using the traffic data in conjunction with the speed/flow relationships.

Elasticities

The elasticities represent the propensities of the various types of traveller to change their volume of travel or to switch mode of travel in response to changes in travel costs and journey times. We derived the elasticities we used from a variety of sources. Graham and Glaister (2002a; 2002b; 2004) provide a survey of evidence on price elasticities of car traffic and freight traffic. The most important of these is a long-run elasticity of car traffic with respect to fuel price of –0.35; that is, if fuel prices rise by 10 per cent, then car traffic will, after a period of full adjustment, fall by 3.5 per cent. Bus elasticities were taken from Dargay and Hanly (1999) and rail elasticities from ATOC (2001). London-specific elasticities are provided by Grayling and Glaister (2000).[1]

---

1   Complete technical information can be found in Glaister and Graham (2003a).

The maps

We illustrate the geographical distribution of the effects we predict our policies to have by means of a series of maps. This can only be a general indication because our model does not contain a representation of the actual road network or the origins and destinations of trips. In outline the maps were constructed as follows.

The data are arranged in 8,960 rows. Each row corresponds to a type of road (1 to 7), in a particular area (1 to 10), in one of the nine regions of England, at some time of the day (divided into eleven periods), and in a busy or non-busy direction.

We developed a correspondence between these rows and the electoral wards of England. We chose to represent two types of effect geographically: changes in traffic volume and changes in traffic speed.

For traffic data we take passenger car units (PCU): a measure of the road space consumed by commercial vehicles and buses relative to the standard passenger car, per hour, for each type of road, averaged over defined periods of the day, and allocate this value to the wards in correspondence to their associated location. At ward level we have information on the length of three road types: motorway, A-road, and B-/minor road. We aggregate the model PCU per hour data (by averaging) for the seven road types to correspond to motorway, A-road and B-/minor road. We then multiply the ward PCU per hour values by the length of each road type in the ward to calculate PCU kilometre per hour values, or, in other words, traffic flows.

For speed data the procedure differs slightly because we have to use weighted averages to account for the fact that speeds are associated with different traffic flows.

Glaister and Graham (2003a) specify these procedures in detail.

Limitations

In implementing our model we have used the best evidence we can find. But many simplifying assumptions have been necessary and our approach does have important limitations.

Our model does not allow travellers to switch travel from one time of day to another, mainly because we did not have an objectively defensible way of modelling this. Our results may therefore exaggerate the overall traffic reduction for a particular level of congestion charge as motorists could switch journeys to times of day when congestion was lower. Or the results may understate the overall traffic reduction from congestion charges at a *particular* time of day as people move their journeys to a less busy time of day. In the longer term this effect may be greater than in the shorter term because, in the longer term, school hours, working hours, etc., can be adjusted to reflect the cost of travelling at different times.

The model features no explicit transport network and makes no attempt to represent origin-to-destination trip patterns. Consequently, we are not able to distinguish between changes in numbers of trips and changes in average trip length; the historically observed responses to changes in costs and prices (the elasticities) are measures of a combination of both phenomena.

Our modelling works throughout in terms of costs and charges per vehicle kilometre and average traffic flows (passenger car units per hour). The model is not capable of accurately representing certain types of charging schemes, such as workplace parking charges, cordon or area schemes. In cordon schemes, vehicles are charged at the moment they cross a cordon bounding a designated area and not for the distance they may travel inside the designated area. In area schemes, a vehicle is liable for a charge if it is used in the designated area at the designated times (whether or not it crosses a cordon), as in the London scheme. Again, the charge may not be related to distance travelled. Proper modelling of these schemes requires a different approach at a finer grain of geographical detail.

Our representation of public transport is less satisfactory than that for road travel. This is because, as we have noted, the available public transport statistics are simply not as good as those we had for road traffic. One particular note of caution should be raised regarding the zero-tax scenario outlined below. In principle subsidies to public transport should have been eliminated entirely, but we found that it is not feasible to do this for bus subsidies by raising fares. We had assumed that all the demand relationships have the property that as a price is increased the responsiveness (elasticity of demand) also increases, to represent the fact that the respective service is becoming less competitive. As a consequence, there comes a point where raising price no longer increases revenue (that is, the revenue is maximised at the point where the elasticity reaches unity). As we have represented them, the economics of the bus industry were so weak that subsidy could not be eliminated at any fare. So bus fares were raised by 20 per cent and 33 per cent in London. Rail fares were raised by 80 per cent.

In the cases of cars, commercial vehicles and buses we have assumed throughout that the number of individuals in each vehicle would stay the same as in the observed base situation. In reality changes in charges would create incentives to increase vehicle occupancies. That could be an important consideration: if occupancies were to increase by 10 per cent then one could carry the same number of individuals using 10 per cent less road space.

The costs that are to be imputed to environmental damage such as air pollution and climate change are uncertain but they are important determinants of the pricing policies considered in this study. We accept the estimates of Sansom et al. (2001) of the several external and environmental costs of transport, summarised in Table 4. We recognise that making these estimates is difficult and different people will come to different conclusions. We use values at the 'low' and the 'high' ends of the ranges to give an indication of how sensitive the policy conclusions might be to different assumptions made about the level of costs that should be imposed upon motorists in respect of environmental externalities. There are also some important factors that have not been – or cannot be – quantified. Some of these omitted factors may be detrimental to the environment or create social costs: for example, severance of communities by roads. Others are beneficial or create social benefits: for example, better accessibility to family, leisure pursuits or employment opportunities. It is not apparent to us that we have necessarily either underestimated or overestimated the external costs and benefits of transport.

As a simplification our modelling in the remainder of this study abstracts from the complication of future growth and analyses the way road user charging policies might have looked had they been imposed in year 2000 conditions. Realistic representation of the future situation is difficult for several reasons. Two of the most important are as follows. First, the growth in traffic would not be geographically uniform. To model this would be outside the scope of this study. Second, there will be increases in the capacity of road and rail networks by 2010, particularly at the places where congestion would become the most severe. Again, modelling these capacity increases fell outside the scope of this study.

Because of traffic growth stimulated by economic growth and falling motoring costs the appropriate charges and the revenue they would generate in, say, 2010 would be substantially greater than those set out in the remainder of this study, and also significantly greater than the revenue likely to be raised through fuel duty under present policies. Naturally, the magnitude of the congestion charges that might be 'justified' by 2010 would be reduced to the extent that more capacity was provided or the underlying fuel taxation was to be increased.

5 ADDING USER CHARGES TO EXISTING TAXES

We have modelled a range of road user charging policies. These include 'revenue-raising' and 'revenue-neutral' charging options and economically efficient pricing. We discuss the main results in Chapters 5 to 7. More detailed results and in-depth discussion can be found in Glaister and Graham (2003a; 2003b) and Graham and Glaister (2003).

In each of Chapters 5 to 7, we use tables similar to Table 5 and Table 6 in this chapter to illustrate the effects of introducing the particular congestion charging regime. Table 5 shows the extent of the change in usage of different modes of transport arising from the imposition of congestion charges followed by changes in costs and subsidies. The transport usage figures are defined as ratios so that 0.5, for example, would illustrate that usage had reduced by 50 per cent.

Table 6, Column (1) shows an estimate of the total reduction in environmental costs as a result of the user charging policy. Column (2) shows benefits accruing to car, bus and rail passengers and to road freight operators (the total of charges paid net of any benefits such as faster journey times arising from the reduced traffic flow). Column (5) shows the direct revenue gain to the Exchequer in terms of the user charges net of any rebates paid to vehicle users. There are additional financial implications for the Exchequer. It is assumed that changes in bus and rail subsidies ultimately pass

Table 5 The result of adding charges to existing taxes

Scenario	Traffic	All passenger km	Car km	Commercial vehicle km	Bus passenger km	Rail passenger km	Car cost £ per km	Bus subsidy £m p.a.	Bus fare (ex London) % change	Rail subsidy £m pa	Rail fare % change
	——— Ratio of flow to the current value ———										
Current (2003)	1	1	1	1	1	1	0.104	1,408	–	1,597	–
Low environmental costs											
Environmental charge	0.94	0.95	0.95	0.94	1.014	1.015	0.116	1,403	0	1,547	0
Environmental charge plus congestion charge	0.91	0.92	0.91	0.90	1.07	1.02	0.132	1,358	0	1,520	0
High environmental costs											
Environmental charge plus congestion charge	0.81	0.87	0.82	0.77	1.09	1.06	0.152	1,390	0	1,447	0

Table 6 Economic evaluation: adding charges to existing taxes (£bn p.a., 2003 prices)

Scenario	Saving in environmental cost	Passenger and freight benefit	Reduction in bus subsidy	Reduction in rail subsidy	Environmental tax, congestion charge revenue & rebates	Net benefit	Tax revenue correction	Net gain to Exchequer	Benefits net of all costs to Exchequer	Weighted average marginal congestion costs (£/vehicle km)
Column reference	(1)	(2)	(3)	(4)	(5)	(6) = (1+2+3+4+5)	(7)	(8) = (3+4+5+7)	(9) = (1+2+8) = (1+2+3+4+5+7)	
Low environmental costs										
Environmental charge	0.54	-4.66	0.01	0.05	5.8	1.74	-1.3	4.56	0.44	0.080
Environmental charge plus congestion charge	0.91	-7.99	0.05	0.08	11.9	4.95	-2.2	9.83	2.75	0.075
High environmental costs										
Environmental charge plus congestion charge	5.04	-15.57	0.05	0.18	19.13	8.83	-4.36	15.0	4.47	0.082

to the Exchequer in full (a positive number in columns (3) and (4) indicates a reduction in subsidy) and that there are changes in fuel tax receipts (above changes in VAT on fuel) because of changes in the volume of fuel purchased (Column (7)). Column (8) summarises the overall Exchequer position. Column (6) shows the net benefit of the road pricing regime. Column (9) shows the benefit net of all costs to the Exchequer.

In this chapter we take current fuel duty and other charges as fixed at today's level and assume that new road user charges are *additional* to them. First we assume that charges are added to reflect the environmental costs of road use only. Then we consider the impact of road user charging when an element reflecting the cost of congestion is added.

Environmental charges

Under this policy an additional charge is made to reflect environmental costs alone (which depend somewhat on vehicle type and location). There are no congestion charges. Low environmental costs are assumed to determine the charge. In this case, where user charging is added to existing road taxes and charges, aggregate traffic and travel are reduced by 5 and 6 per cent respectively. There is some increase in bus and rail travel.

Table 6 shows an environmental cost saving of about £0.5 billion per annum and an increase in Exchequer revenues of about £4.5 billion per annum. This illustrates how a charge can be used to address concerns about environmental damage. Of course, the critical issue is the set of estimates used for the per-vehicle kilometre environmental damage costs. But it is not the case, of course, that the existence of environmental damage should lead policy towards reducing traffic at all costs – unless one believes that the environmental costs are unbounded. Note that the environmental charges also achieve benefits through reducing congestion because they reduce overall traffic flow.

Environmental charges and congestion charges

We now make a further addition of a charge fully to reflect the incremental congestion cost that each vehicle inflicts on all others. In this scenario every type of road user bears an additional charge per vehicle kilometre matching the estimated environmental damage it causes and a congestion charge corresponding to the total congestion costs that each additional vehicle kilometre imposes on all other traffic.

Table 6 shows that, using the low environmental damage costs to determine the charges, this set of charges would yield extra direct revenue of £11.9 billion per annum, some improvement of bus and rail finances and an overall increase in the Exchequer revenue of £9.8 billion per annum.

In some congested places the charges are high and the reduction in traffic is substantial. But in many places and for much of the time there is little congestion, so the increase in charges is only the relatively small environmental tax. The net result is that this level of charges, that is charges that reflect all the costs of road use, involves a reduction of only 9 per cent in overall traffic levels – indicating the extent to which congestion is a localised problem.

Maps 3 and 4 show speed and traffic changes and how the speed and traffic changes vary across the country. Note that in the Greater London area the inner and outer areas are a darker shade of blue than the central area. This feature is also found in the maps

Figure 4   **Current fuel tax rates, environmental charges and congestion charges (low environmental costs)**
% of cases

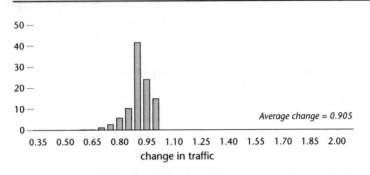

change in traffic

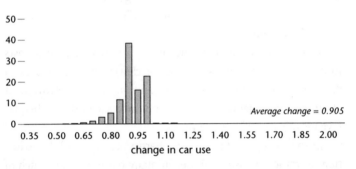

change in car use

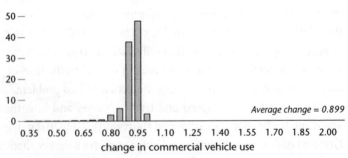

change in commercial vehicle use

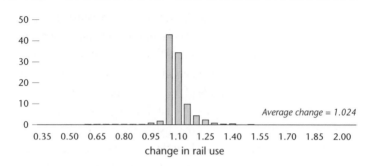

Average change = 1.024

change in rail use

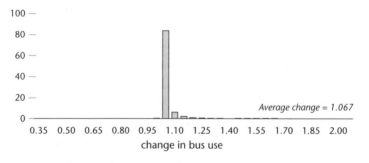

Average change = 1.067

change in bus use

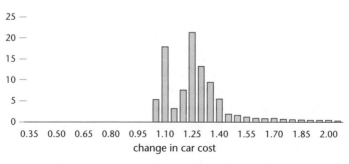

change in car cost

illustrating other policy scenarios, and it indicates that traffic congestion and the benefits of congestion charging are greater in those inner and outer areas than in the central area, where congestion charging was actually introduced in February 2003. This reflects the common experience of London conditions, and it suggests that, if a way can be found to achieve it, the strongest candidate in England for congestion charging would be inner-London, or possibly the whole of the Greater London area.

Figure 4 shows the impact of charging in greater detail. Each panel is a histogram showing the distribution of the 8,960 cases (as explained in Chapter 4) with respect to the variable indicated. These different cases represent different times of the day, geographical areas, etc. For example, if we take the third figure in the second column of Figure 4, this indicates the cost of using a car in all the different 8,960 scenarios that were modelled. The figure shows a change in car cost represented by a ratio (1.0 implies no change, 0.9 a 10 per cent decrease, and 1.1 a 10 per cent increase, for example). In many cases the cost of using a car increases by a factor of between 1.1 and 1.3 (that is, between 10 and 30 per cent), mainly reflecting the environmental charges. There are cases where the charges on cars would increase by a much greater factor (up to a factor of 3, at which point we capped the cost increases). These represent a small portion of the affected traffic, however. There are also some cases (for example, in respect of journeys in rural areas) where there are no increases in motoring costs. There might be some cases where the benefits from a reduction in journey time outweighed any increase in cost. More generally, we can see the distribution of outcomes arising from the imposition of road user charges.

Table 5 shows that environmental charges at the low level together with congestion charges would reduce overall traffic by

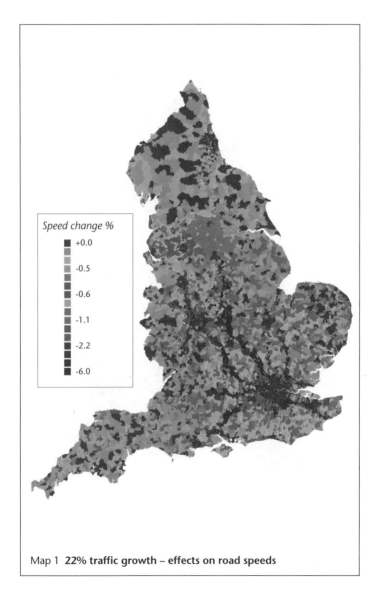

Map 1 **22% traffic growth – effects on road speeds**

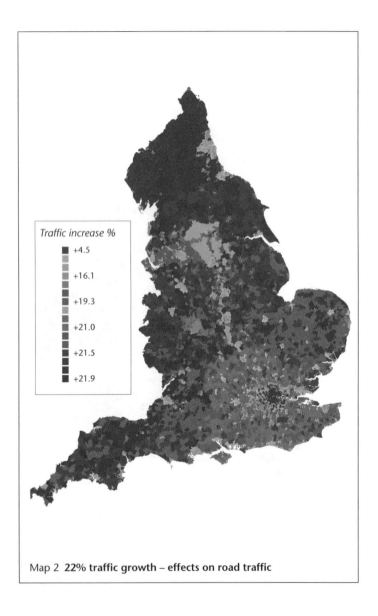

Traffic increase %

■ +4.5

■ +16.1

■ +19.3

■ +21.0

■ +21.5

■ +21.9

Map 2 **22% traffic growth – effects on road traffic**

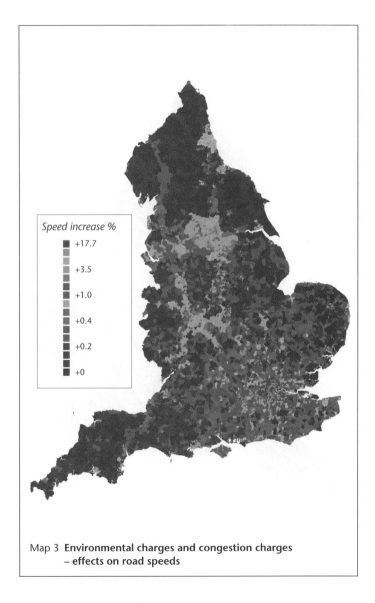

Map 3 **Environmental charges and congestion charges
– effects on road speeds**

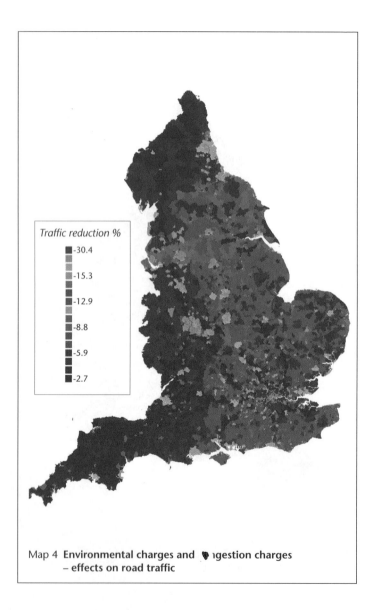

Traffic reduction %

- -30.4
- -15.3
- -12.9
- -8.8
- -5.9
- -2.7

Map 4 **Environmental charges and congestion charges
– effects on road traffic**

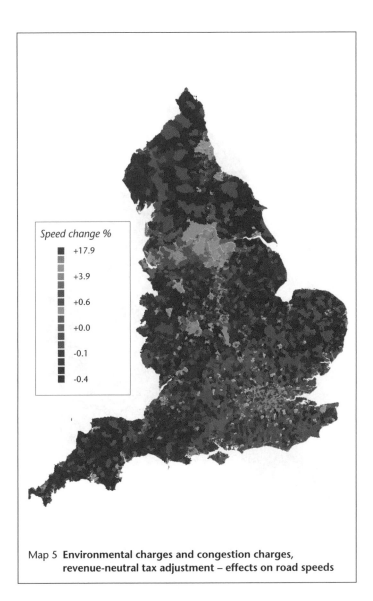

Map 5 **Environmental charges and congestion charges,
revenue-neutral tax adjustment – effects on road speeds**

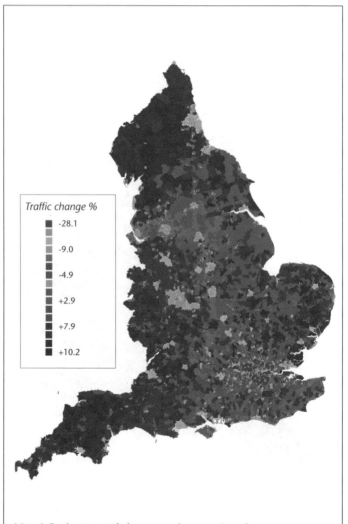

Traffic change %

- -28.1
- -9.0
- -4.9
- +2.9
- +7.9
- +10.2

Map 6 Environmental charges and congestion charges,
      revenue-neutral tax adjustment - effects on road traffic

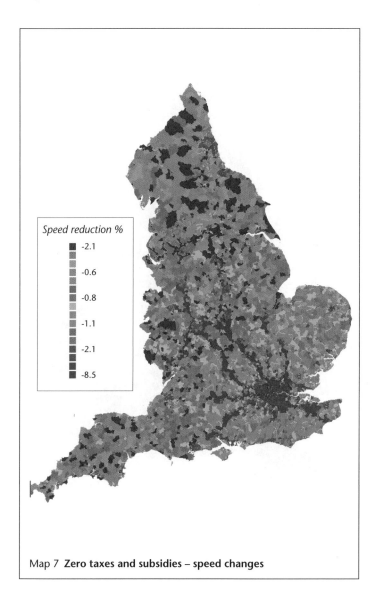

Speed reduction %

- -2.1
- -0.6
- -0.8
- -1.1
- -2.1
- -8.5

Map 7 **Zero taxes and subsidies – speed changes**

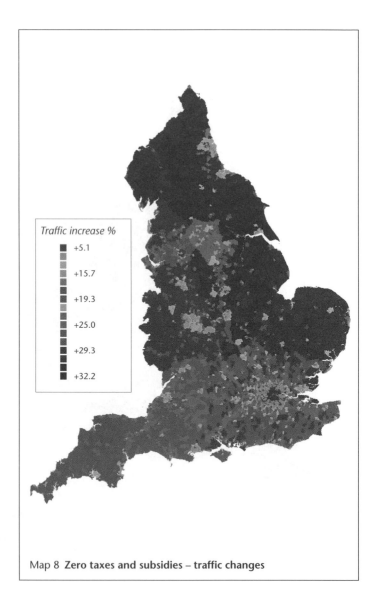

Traffic increase %

+5.1
+15.7
+19.3
+25.0
+29.3
+32.2

Map 8 **Zero taxes and subsidies – traffic changes**

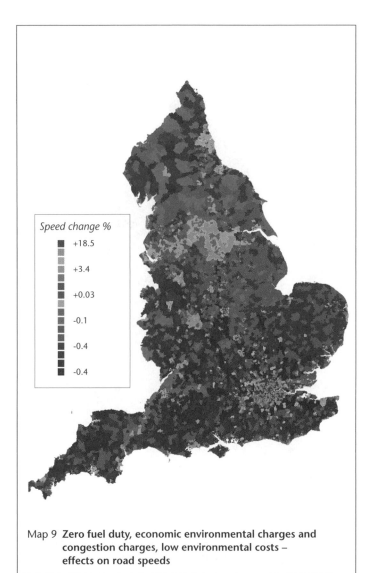

Map 9 **Zero fuel duty, economic environmental charges and congestion charges, low environmental costs – effects on road speeds**

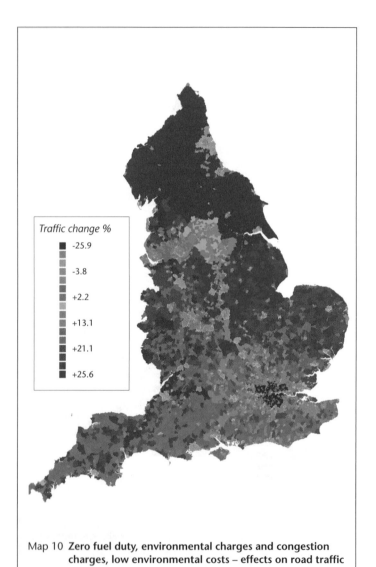

Traffic change %

-25.9
-3.8
+2.2
+13.1
+21.1
+25.6

Map 10 **Zero fuel duty, environmental charges and congestion charges, low environmental costs – effects on road traffic**

about 9 per cent whilst environmental charges alone would reduce it by 6 per cent. Although environmental charges are relatively small compared with the congestion charges in highly congested areas, congestion charges apply only at relatively few times in a few places whilst environmental charges are universal.

The overall evaluation of benefits in Table 6 shows that net of costs there is a gain of £2.75 billion per annum, with the overall disbenefit to vehicle users, passengers and freight of about £8 billion per annum being offset by environmental benefits, improved public transport finances and increased tax revenues (which are largely a reflection of the value of improved travel conditions).

This policy of environmental taxation and congestion charging could be combined with an almost complete removal of the annual vehicle licensing charge (Vehicle Excise Duty, VED – the tax disc). That would leave a net increase in road taxation of the order of £7 billion per annum because total VED revenue is about £5 billion per annum (that is, £11.9 billion in Table 6 minus £5 billion). Thus the policy could involve moving taxation away from fixed charges on ownership towards charges for use. Policies that change the form of road user charging and taxation rather than imposing charging on top of existing systems are discussed in Chapters 6 and 7.

Tables 5 and 6 also show the corresponding results using the high environmental costs. Now overall traffic falls by 19 per cent rather than 9 per cent. The net gain to the Exchequer rises to £15 billion per annum from £10 billion per annum, and the saving in environmental costs increases from £0.91 billion per annum to £5.04 billion per annum. These differences reflect the fact that, as shown in Table 4, the high environmental cost estimates are significantly greater than the low ones, particularly in respect of air pollution and climate change.

6 REVENUE-NEUTRAL ENVIRONMENTAL AND CONGESTION CHARGES

This policy preserves the same structure of taxes and charges as in the previous chapter, but makes a rebate per vehicle kilometre so that the overall direct charge revenue is unchanged from today's level (and there is an increase in total fuel tax take of £0.6 billion per annum because there is an overall increase in the volume of fuel consumed). Overall, this has the effect of maintaining revenue from road users at approximately the current level. Road users are charged at the margin for the congestion and environmental damage that they cause but charges per kilometre are then reduced at a uniform rate to leave total revenue to the Exchequer unchanged. Thus there are differential charges to reflect environmental damage and congestion because the rebate paid to motorists is based only on total distance travelled. Throughout this chapter and the next one we assume that VED (the tax disc) is left unchanged as a simplification. As we noted in the previous chapter, it would undoubtedly have to be considered as a part of any practical package of changes to taxes and charges. Indeed, the per kilometre passenger rebate that has been assumed in this chapter could be replaced by a removal of VED and a reduction in fuel tax to produce revenue neutrality.

The results are displayed in Figures 5 and 6 and Maps 5 and 6. The effects on traffic are quantified in Tables 7 and 8. This scenario is particularly interesting in that it achieves a redistribution of

Table 7 **Results of revenue-neutral environmental and congestion charges**

Scenario	Traffic	All passenger km	Car km	Commercial vehicle km	Bus passenger km	Rail passenger km	Car cost £ per km	Bus subsidy	Bus fare (ex London)	Rail subsidy	Rail fare
		——— Ratio of flow to the current value ———						£m p.a.	% change	£m pa	% change
Current (2003)	1	1	1	1	1	1	0.104	1,408	–	1,597	–
Low environmental costs											
Environmental charges and congestion charges, revenue neutral	1.01	1.04	1.01	1.01	1.05	0.99	0.103	1,371	0	1,633	0

Table 8 Economic evaluation: revenue-neutral environmental and congestion charges (£bn p.a., 2003 prices)

Scenario	Saving in environmental cost	Passenger and freight benefit	Reduction in bus subsidy	Reduction in rail subsidy	Environmental tax, congestion charge revenue & rebates	Net benefit	Tax revenue correction	Net gain to Exchequer	Benefits net of all costs to Exchequer	Weighted average marginal congestion costs (£/vehicle km)
Column reference	(1)	(2)	(3)	(4)	(5)	(6) = (1+2+3+4+5)	(7)	(8) = (3+4+5+7)	(9) = (1+2+8) = (1+2+3+4+5+7)	
Low environmental charges										
Environmental charges and congestion charges, revenue neutral	0.28	0.88	0.04	-0.04	0	1.16	0.6	0.6	1.76	0.068

traffic away from congested times and places and away from those areas where environmental damage is greatest, while leaving total tax and charge revenues largely unchanged and accommodating a slight *increase* in overall traffic.

Table 7 shows how the overall effect on traffic volume is broadly neutral but the histograms in Figure 5 show a considerable dispersion about the average. While many cases (that is, times and places) would experience only a small increase or decrease in traffic, there are substantial numbers of cases that would enjoy a 20 to 30 per cent reduction – the more congested urban areas – and substantial numbers of cases that would experience 10 to 15 per cent increases – the less congested times and rural areas. The drivers at less congested times and in rural areas would benefit from the rebate designed to ensure revenue neutrality but would pay very low user charges. The overall effect on commercial vehicles is less variable than that on private cars, but the two lighter classes of commercial vehicle are more likely to enjoy a cost reduction than the heavy articulated lorries. Presumably this is because the heaviest vehicles, which consume a great deal of fuel, suffer more from the environmental charge and also use the more congested roads on average. There is a broadly neutral overall effect on rail travel with small reductions at many times and places balanced by larger increases over a wide range of times and places. There is an overall 5 per cent increase in bus travel.

Map 5 shows the geographical incidence of this policy in terms of speed changes and Map 6 shows the geographical distribution of traffic reduction. Traffic is most reduced in the big conurbations (coloured blue in Map 6) and it increases most in the country areas (coloured red), most notably in the North of England. Much of the central part of England outside the big cities is brownish,

Figure 5   **Environmental charges and congestion charges;
revenue-neutral tax adjustment (low environment costs)**
% of cases

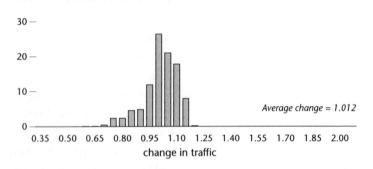

Average change = 1.012

change in traffic

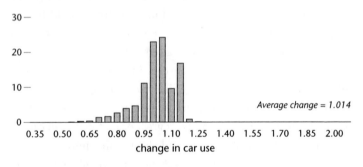

Average change = 1.014

change in car use

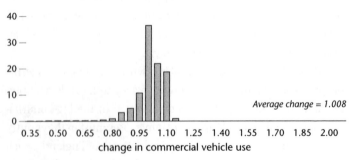

Average change = 1.008

change in commercial vehicle use

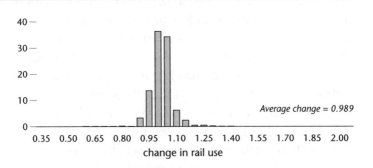

Average change = 0.989

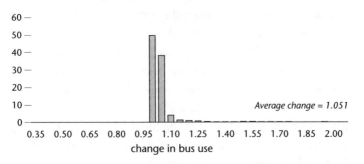

Average change = 1.051

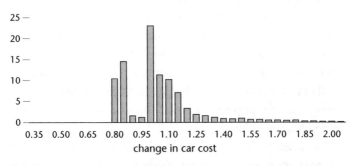

indicating little traffic volume change. Map 5 shows how the big cities enjoy a substantial speed improvement. Interestingly, many of the places that have the biggest traffic volume increase (such as the North of England) have little or no speed reduction – because they are areas with spare capacity and therefore little congestion. Thus many motorists will enjoy a substantial speed improvement, there will be very little reduction in traffic speeds in other areas and motorists as a whole are not financially worse off. The redistribution of traffic from congested to non-congested areas, facilitated by this charging scheme, has clear economic benefits. This scenario illustrates the proposition that, at today's overall rates of fuel tax, motorists in city areas are undercharged for the congestion and environmental damage they cause, while those in country areas are significantly overcharged.

Compared with the policy that is not tax-revenue-neutral the overall net economic benefit is reduced from £2.8 billion per annum to £1.8 billion per annum. This is mainly because traffic is reduced less so there are fewer environmental benefits. The rebate ensures that many motorists are not quite paying the full marginal economic cost of making journeys, although if the rebate were in a different form (for example, through reducing vehicle excise duty) the overall economic benefits could be greater. The use of the per passenger kilometre rebate has the advantage, however, of leaving passengers and freight users as a whole better off by £0.9 billion per annum, while generating a small improvement to the Exchequer finances. Further, the costs arising from the pressure to provide more road capacity would be significantly reduced.

Thus, here we have a set of road user charges that are clearly not optimal from an economic point of view. Charges are imposed that do reflect all the costs of road use. Existing charges are retained, however – which they should not be in an optimal system – and a uniform rebate is offered – which also should not happen in an optimal system. Nevertheless, this chapter does show that, even with this system, there are considerable economic benefits. If politicians feel the need to 'buy off' affected groups through other tax changes, even if this undermines some of the economic objectives of the policy, there can still be considerable economic benefits compared with the current situation.

7 FULLY EFFICIENT TAXES AND SUBSIDIES

The current set of taxes has developed over the decades and has no economic rationale. There is no reason to expect that the total tax revenue over and above that which would result from the standard rates levied on other sectors of the economy has any justification in terms of external damage costs. The various taxes imposed upon motorists have not been developed to ensure that the total costs of motoring reflect the marginal social cost of vehicle use. In this section we derive a set of taxes and subsidies built upon fundamental economic principles.

Zero special taxes and subsidies

First we investigate what might happen if the transport sector were subject to the same rates of taxation (and subsidy) as are most other sectors of the economy. In this scenario, motoring costs do not reflect congestion and environmental costs; rather motoring is treated like bus use, so that the car user pays only the private marginal costs (plus Value Added Tax) of car use. As far as is practically possible, subsidies are removed from public transport.

As part of this scenario, 67 per cent of fuel duty is rebated to those who pay it, so that fuel bears, approximately, the standard rate of Value Added Tax. An attempt is also made to remove

Table 9 Fully efficient taxes and subsidies

Scenario	Traffic	All passenger km	Car km	Commercial vehicle km	Bus passenger km	Rail passenger km	Car cost £ per km	Bus subsidy £m p.a.	Bus fare (ex London) % change	Rail subsidy £m pa	Rail fare % change
	Ratio of flow to the current value[1]										
Current (2003)	1	1	1	1	1	1	0.104	1,408	-	1,597	-
Low environmental costs											
Zero tax	1.26	1.19	1.22	1.31	1.04	0.85	0.061	917	+20	994	+80
Zero tax, environmental charges & congestion charges	1.12	1.06	1.09	1.16	1.12	0.67	0.093	793	+20	914	+80
Zero tax, environmental charges & congestion charges & revenue-neutral mark-up	1.04	1.00	1.02	1.06	1.13	0.69	0.108	777	+20	822	80
High environmental costs											
Zero tax, environmental charges & congestion charges	1.01	0.98	1.0	1.0	1.14	0.69	0.111	783	+20	807	+80
Zero tax, environmental charges & congestion charges & revenue-neutral mark-up	1.04	1.01	1.03	1.04	1.13	0.68	0.106	787	+20	844	80

1 For example, a ratio of 1.2 would normally be interpreted as a 20 per cent increase and a ratio of 0.94 as a 6 per cent reduction.

subsidies to public transport. In fact the commercial position of the bus and rail industries is so poor that it is not sensible to attempt to make them break even. It probably would not be feasible for them to break even at any set of economic prices charged to customers. In any case, any attempt to move too far towards a break-even position has the consequence of causing almost all services to be cut. We therefore compromised on this aspect of the zero taxes and subsidies scenario and increased bus fares by 20 per cent generally, and by 33 per cent in London, where the bus market is stronger. We increased rail fares by 80 per cent, at which point the characteristics of our model imply that rail revenues would be approximately maximised.

The cost to the Exchequer of this scenario is £20.4 billion per annum (shown in Table 10): arising from cutting road taxes, offset slightly by the reduction in public transport subsidies. The corresponding changes in traffic volumes and speeds are shown in Maps 7 and 8.

It can be seen that there are traffic increases and speed reductions in all areas. This is because there have been unambiguous reductions in the cost of motoring. Table 9 shows a 22 per cent increase in car use and a 31 per cent increase in commercial vehicle use. There is a considerable cost saving for car users, shown in Table 10, column (5).

Zero taxes and subsidies plus environmental and congestion charges

We now build on this 'zero tax' base by imposing both environmental charges and congestion charges so that the motorist pays the marginal social cost of car use. In principle this creates

Table 10 Economic evaluation: fully efficient taxes and subsidies (£bn p.a., 2003 prices)

Scenario	Saving in environmental cost	Passenger and environmental freight benefit	Reduction in bus subsidy	Reduction in rail subsidy	Environmental tax, congestion charge revenue & rebates	Net benefit	Tax revenue correction	Net gain to Exchequer	Benefits net of all costs to Exchequer	Weighted average marginal congestion costs (£/vehicle km)
Column reference	(1)	(2)	(3)	(4)	(5)	(6) = (1+2+3+4+5)	(7)	(8) = (3+4+5+7)	(9) = (1+2+8) = (1+2+3+4+5+7)	
Low environmental costs										
Zero tax	-1.63	18.03	0.49	0.60	-27.5	-10.01	+6.0	-20.41	-4.01	0.010
Zero tax, environmental charges & congestion charges	-0.40	6.81	0.62	0.68	-7.9	-0.19	+2.8	-3.80	2.61	0.062
Zero tax, environmental charges & congestion charges & revenue-neutral mark-up	0.32	0.15	0.63	0.77	0	1.87	+1.0	2.40	2.87	0.064
High environmental costs										
Zero tax, environmental charges & congestion charges	1.60	-1.92	0.63	0.77	3.03	4.11	+0.18	4.61	4.29	0.065
Zero tax, environmental charges & congestion charges & revenue-neutral mark-up	0.79	0.72	0.62	0.75	0	2.88	0.9	2.27	3.78	0.070

a 'proper' set of road charges, based on economic principles, irrespective of where they happen to be set today.

If environmental charges are set at the low level, then compared with today's levels, it costs the Exchequer £7.9 billion per annum in rebates of fuel duty, etc., and overall Exchequer revenues are reduced by £3.8 billion per annum after allowing for the revenue from user charges. Traffic increases by 12 per cent, private car use by 6 per cent and commercial vehicle use by 16 per cent. The subsidy to the bus industry falls from £1,408 million per annum to £793 million per annum, and that for the rail industry falls from £1,597 million per annum to £914 million per annum: see Table 9. Overall, as shown in Table 10, column (2), there is a benefit to passengers and freight of £6.8 billion per annum, although there is a small environmental damage cost of £0.4 billion per annum.

These results illustrate the proposition that, on these assumptions, if charges were to be set in accordance with economic efficiency principles, rather than retaining charges that have come about largely by historical accident, then road users would pay less than they do today. Average money costs per car kilometre would fall from 10.4 pence to 9.3 pence. There would be a net increase in economic efficiency. Indeed, there would be a general increase in traffic speeds which would be substantial in some areas. The impacts on traffic speeds and volumes are far from equally distributed geographically, as Maps 9 and 10 indicate. Traffic is reduced in areas where vehicles impose a high marginal cost currently and increased in other areas. The redistribution of traffic is one aspect of the increased economic efficiency from this set of charges.

Tables 9 and 10 show that the situation would be different assuming the high environmental costs. Rather than a net loss to the Exchequer of £3.8 billion per annum there would be a net gain of £4.61 billion. Of course, this reflects the more aggressive stance towards charging for environmental effects: there is an estimated environmental gain of £1.6 billion per annum against the current base compared with a £0.4 billion per annum loss using this set of charging principles but with low environmental costs. Average money costs per car kilometre would rise from 10.4 pence to 11 pence.

It turns out that if we assume the low environmental costs then the 'proper' set of road user charges would yield £3.8 billion per annum less than today's revenue from fuel duty (Table 10, Column (8)), and if we assume the high environmental costs then they would yield £4.61 billion per annum more. Therefore, in terms of our model, the answer to the question as to whether road users are *currently* paying too much or too little overall depends upon what view is taken about where the 'correct' environmental charges lie between our two extremes. Nevertheless, whichever set of environmental charges is deemed appropriate, there are economic benefits from changing the charging structure for motorists.

These conclusions relate to traffic conditions as they were in the year 2000. Ten years later, after the traffic growth we discuss above, the total payments would be substantially higher under all sets of assumptions about the environmental costs.

In considering these results it should be remembered that our model also does not attempt to represent any propensity to change the time of day at which travel takes place. In practice there would be a tendency to retime journeys in order to avoid the higher rates of charge at the busiest times. This would foster more efficient use of the available network capacity, reduce the severity of the peak charges and allow some traffic to continue rather than being deterred altogether. It should also be noted that our model does not allow for any increased car sharing, which might bring about further reductions in car use in congested areas without reducing total passenger kilometres travelled.

It is also worth noting that, although we have not done the simulations for this case, it would appear that using a mid-range estimate for the environmental costs would probably produce a set of charges that are approximately revenue-neutral. While not having any particular economic significance, it may be of political significance that a change in the structure of road user charges could, in fact, be engineered so that it is approximately revenue-neutral yet, at the same time, brings about significant economic advantages.

The previous cases represent an idealised situation. In practice a revenue-neutral scenario might be more politically attractive. As noted, using a mid-range environmental cost estimate might produce this outcome, but we addressed the revenue-neutral case by imposing an equiproportionate mark-up or mark-down so that the direct effect on Exchequer finances is neutral, relative to today's circumstances. The required mark-up was a factor of about 2 for the low environmental cost case and the mark-down was a factor of 0.83 (that is, a reduction of about 17 per cent) for the high environmental cost case.

The low environmental costs case combined with the mark-up to make the new regime revenue neutral gives the best overall net benefit of all the low environmental cost scenarios we considered, at £2.9 billion per annum.[1] There is a net gain to the Exchequer

---

1   The revenue-neutral case (Row 3 of Table 10) appears to show a better overall economic return than the revenue-unconstrained case (Row 2). On first principles one would expect the reverse. This may be a consequence of the 'capping' that has been applied to ensure that no road user type experiences more than

of £2.4 billion per annum, largely due to a marked improvement in bus and rail finances (this, in turn, is partly due to the fares increases of 20 per cent and 80 per cent respectively). There is a reduction in environmental damage valued at £0.32 billion per annum. Passengers and freight users are slightly better off by £0.15 billion per annum.

Under the assumption of high environmental costs the estimated environmental savings are greater, as would be expected. There is a residual net gain to the Exchequer of £2.3 billion per annum and an overall economic benefit of £3.8 billion per annum when the charging regime is constrained to be revenue neutral. This is less than the overall benefit of £4.3 billion per annum under the revenue-unconstrained case. Of course, there is less of a tendency to reduce charges in non-urban areas than under the low environmental cost case.

a threefold increase in money costs per vehicle kilometre. This means that the 'optimum' (Row 2) is, in fact, not a full economic optimum. Note that in the case with high environmental costs the relationship is as would be expected (Row 3 of Table 10 has a better return than Row 4). The scenario of environmental congestion charges added to today's tax levels (Row 3 of Table 6) yields higher net benefits still. This result is misleading, however, because it assumes lower public transport fares and therefore rail fares closer to the (artificial) zero marginal cost of railways.

8 HOW WIDELY SHOULD CHARGING BE IMPLEMENTED?

This chapter concerns the balance between location-specific charging and charging through the conventional fuel duty, bearing in mind the costs of introducing and administering new charging systems. Throughout our work we have given little attention to the vital issue of what a practical scheme might look like. A full treatment would require the inclusion of capital and operating costs of suitable technologies. Newbery (2002) discusses some of the subtleties of an economically effective design for a real scheme.

It is easy to see that there may well be a case for considering a scheme that does not attempt to cover the whole country. As a charging scheme is extended progressively to less dense areas the administrative costs are likely to rise while the traffic affected and the economically efficient prices that road users should pay – and hence the revenue – are likely to rise much less rapidly. In this chapter we consider, in general terms, the merits of implementing a charging scheme for the whole country relative to a partial scheme that would target those areas where the problems are most severe.

The issue of initial investment and ongoing administration costs is crucial, as illustrated by the experience of the scheme introduced in London in February 2003. As we noted above, a substantial part of the expected revenues is consumed by the capital and operating costs of the scheme. This does not necessarily mean that the London scheme was not worthwhile, but it does suggest that a sensible scheme covering a wider and less congested area would have to have much lower costs if it were to remain worthwhile.

The relationship between benefits and coverage

The spread of costs and economies of scale will depend on the technology used. This in turn will have implications for the coverage. With camera-based technology the case for limited geographical coverage may be stronger than with technology involving satellite-based geographical positioning systems. With the latter, the marginal cost of extending charging to areas with less dense traffic may be considerably reduced, even though cameras and other roadside equipment will be essential in support of any satellite-based system and for enforcement.

In this chapter we illustrate how revenues and benefits might vary with different scales of implementation, using the scenario of low environmental costs and using congestion charges in addition to today's taxes without any offsetting rebates (the policy discussed in Chapter 5). Since this assumes that environmental charges should be added to today's fuel taxes, where only a partial location-specific scheme is introduced governments might seek to make an approximate environmental charge by means of an increase in fuel duty. If this were done then the areas where location-specific charging was judged to be worthwhile would be fewer. Of course, this would fail to reflect geographical or temporal variations in environmental damage costs.

The following calculations are only indicative: an accurate picture would require more analysis and information on the costs of the proposed technology.

Charging thresholds

First, in view of the inevitable costs of implementing a charging system, it is natural to think in terms of not implementing it in circumstances where the charge rate would be low. In Figure 6 we progressively raise the threshold on rates of charge per car kilometre below which no charging would be implemented. If this threshold were at a high level (for example, 25 pence per kilometre) large numbers of journeys would be exempt from the charge: only cars travelling in very congested areas would pay. If the threshold were at a low level (for example, 5 pence per kilometre) relatively few journeys would be exempt from the charge: perhaps only those in rural areas. As more people are exempted, the environmental benefits of charging shrink and there is also a reduction in revenue from the charge. At the same time the disbenefits to travellers from charging fall. The effect of exempting more people as the charging threshold is increased is shown in Figure 6. For the purpose of this exercise we have neglected the changes in public transport subsidies and any correction due to changes in the duty on fuel because the quantity of fuel consumed would change.

The figure indicates that, as the very lowest rates of charge are waived, there is a rapid fall in revenues, environmental savings and also disbenefits. The net benefit falls but somewhat less rapidly. This is because the environmental charges apply at relatively low rates in all places and times – even on routes that are not very congested. Once this basic charge in respect of environmental costs has been forgone then raising the threshold below which charging does not take place makes little difference between about 5 pence per car kilometre and 16 pence per car kilometre: the net benefits are remarkably stable. This suggests that, unless a decision were taken to implement universal charging, there would

Figure 6   **The effects of waiving low rates of charge**

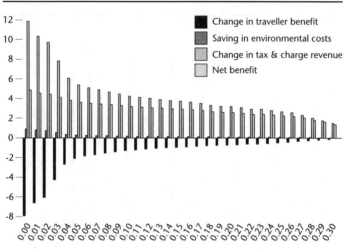

be little point in incurring the costs involved in levying charges below about 16 pence per car kilometre.

Figure 7 indicates how these results are generated. It illustrates, for the nine regions, the number of cases (times and places) in which cars will pay a charge if the threshold below which no charge is levied is set at different rates. As the threshold is raised from zero, progressively fewer cases are caught by the charge – the number of cases being represented by the horizontal axis in each diagram. Thus, if the threshold were zero, journeys at all times and in all places would incur at least the environmental charge, and they all appear as points along the horizontal axis of Figure 7. As the threshold is raised, uncongested places fall out of the scope of charging and their corresponding points disappear from the diagram. Thus, for the more rural, less congested regions the

Figure 7 **Rates of charge by region**
£ per car km

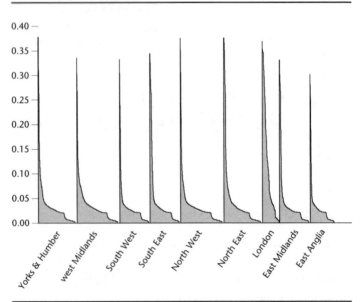

amount of grey reduces rapidly as one moves up the vertical axis. At the other extreme, when the threshold is high, only heavily congested times and places are caught, so a thin spike indicates that a high rate of charge would apply in relatively few circumstances. Note how the area for London is fatter at the higher rates of charge than for the other regions – reflecting the more pervasive nature of the congestion problem in the London area. In London, there are large numbers of situations in which cars pay high charges. This contrasts with East Anglia, for example, where there are few cases in which a charge of more than 10p per car km is levied.

Of course, the design would have to take account of the

geographical location of the places where it would be worthwhile to charge.

Geographical coverage

Figure 8 shows the effect of increasing the coverage of the charge over different types of area. At the left-hand side of the figure, charging applies only to central London; then inner and outer London are included, showing how very much larger a full London scheme would be in terms of revenues and net benefits; then the conurbations are included; then the big urban areas. Whereas revenues increase steadily, so do disbenefits to road users, with the consequence that the net benefit changes little beyond the point at which the biggest urban areas are included (indicated by area types 1–6).

In geographical terms a choice of the degree of coverage would involve trading increasing costs against increasing Exchequer revenues (if that is the main concern) or against net benefit (if the concern is with economic efficiency). A further important consideration would be the savings in capital expenditure for new road capacity that would be avoided by the introduction of a charging scheme.

In order to investigate this further we have classified the charging regime by road type and by area type, as shown in Tables 11 to 13. In each case the calculations were performed once assuming that the appropriate charges would be collected on all roads at all times, and once assuming that charges would be made only where the charge for cars would be in excess of 5 pence per kilometre, thus removing the need to levy charges at quiet times of the day and in uncongested circumstances.

Figure 8   **The effects of extending charging from central London to less urbanised areas**
£bn p.a.

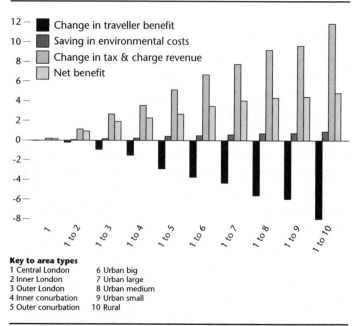

Key:
■ Change in traveller benefit
■ Saving in environmental costs
■ Change in tax & charge revenue
□ Net benefit

X-axis: 1, 1 to 2, 1 to 3, 1 to 4, 1 to 5, 1 to 6, 1 to 7, 1 to 8, 1 to 9, 1 to 10

Key to area types

1 Central London	6 Urban big
2 Inner London	7 Urban large
3 Outer London	8 Urban medium
4 Inner conurbation	9 Urban small
5 Outer conurbation	10 Rural

The 'revenue' is that taken from road users on the respective road type within the stated area types. It shows the areas and road types that would generate the greatest part of the revenues. The 'charge per PCU km' is the average charge paid by those required to pay. The '% change in national traffic' is the change in traffic on the respective road type within the stated area types expressed as a percentage of the total national traffic: so this column shows the breakdown of the total traffic reduction achieved by type of road. Finally, '% national traffic paying' shows the proportion of the national traffic that is being asked to pay anything on the respective road type within the stated area types.

Table 13 shows that the most important road type is type 5, principal A-roads, accounting for £4.48 billion out of the total of £11.54 billion revenues if all area types and road types were to be charged.

Comparing Table 13 with Table 12 indicates that excluding rural and small urban areas (area types 9 and 10) reduces the proportion of the traffic being charged from 92 per cent to 45 per cent, but only reduces the revenues from £11.54 billion per annum to £9.22 billion per annum. Imposing the threshold of 5 pence per car kilometre further reduces the revenue to £5.34 billion per annum, but this means that only about 10 per cent of the traffic is experiencing any charge at all. This would achieve a 2 per cent reduction in national traffic, but a much higher proportionate reduction of traffic in the congested circumstances where charges would apply (e.g. busy times of day, busy areas, etc). In this latter case, the charges (where they are levied) range from 6 pence per car kilometre on urban unclassified roads, through 8 pence on motorways to 16 pence on urban A-roads and 22 pence on urban trunk roads.

In Table 11 only London, the conurbations and big urban areas are included in the charging operation. If the threshold were to apply the revenue would be over £4 billion per annum, but only 8 per cent of national traffic would experience charging. Rates of charge are similar to the previous case.

We cannot draw any conclusions as to how extensively charging should be applied from this analysis alone. It is clear, however, that a considerable benefit can arise from levying

Table 11 **Revenues and charges by road type: area types 1–6**

Road type	Revenue	Charge per PCU km	% change in national traffic	% of national traffic paying	Revenue	Charge per PCU km	% change in national traffic	% of national traffic paying
	£ bn p.a.	Pence	%	%	£ bn p.a.	Pence	%	%
		No threshold				Threshold is 5p per PCU km		
1	0.2	1	-0.3	5	0.01	8	-0.01	0.04
4	1.81	14	-0.64	4	1.59	23	-0.42	2
5	2.61	8	-1.63	9	1.84	15	-0.76	4
6	1.17	9	-0.82	4	0.90	13	-0.55	2
7	0.90	4	-0.94	7	0.08	6	-0.07	0.4
Totals	**6.71**		**-4.33**	**29**	**4.42**		**-1.81**	**8**

Table 12 **Revenues and charges by road type: area types 1–8**

Road type	Revenue	Charge per PCU km	% change in national traffic	% of national traffic paying	Revenue	Charge per PCU km	% change in national traffic	% of national traffic paying
	£ bn p.a.	Pence	%	%	£t bn p.a.	Pence	%	%
		No threshold				Threshold is 5p per PCU km		
1	0.22	1	-0.25	5	0.01	8	-0.01	0.04
4	2.28	11	-0.95	6	1.84	22	-0.52	2
5	3.76	7	-2.46	15	2.39	16	-0.94	4
6	1.62	7	-1.26	7	1.02	11	-0.65	3
7	1.34	3	-1.42	12	0.08	6	-0.07	0.38
Totals	**9.22**		**6.34**	**45**	**5.34**		**7.19**	**10**

Table 13 Revenues and charges by road type: all area types

Road type	Revenue £ bn p.a.	Charge per PCU km Pence	% change in national traffic %	% of national traffic paying %	Revenue £ bn p.a.	Charge per PCU km Pence	% change in national traffic %	% of national traffic paying %
	No threshold				Threshold is 5p per PCU km			
1	0.74	1	-0.82	24	0.01	8	-0.01	0.04
4	2.69	8	-1.43	10	1.87	21	-0.53	3
5	4.48	5	-3.37	25	2.40	16	-0.94	4
6	1.87	4	-1.57	11	1.04	11	-0.67	3
7	1.76	2	-1.94	22	0.08	6	-0.07	0.38
Totals	**11.54**		**-9.13**	**92**	**5.4**		**-2.22**	**10**

Key to road types

Road type	London and conurbations	Other urban	Rural
1	Motorway	N/A	Motorway
2	N/A	N/A	Trunk Dual A
3	N/A	N/A	Principal Dual A
4	Trunk A	Trunk A	Trunk Single A

Road type	London and conurbations	Other urban	Rural
5	Principal A	Principal A	Principal Single A
6	B and C	B and C	B
7	Unclassified	Unclassified	C & Unclassified

Road types 2 and 3 are rural roads with generally light traffic and they are excluded from Tables 11, 12 and 13

charges in particular areas, on particular road types and where charges should be above a given threshold. Thus partial charging schemes can be useful. They are most useful where they give rise to limited traffic displacement to areas that are not part of the charging scheme. In order to draw firm conclusions, we would need to compare the incremental costs of extending charging schemes with the incremental economic benefits. With some technologies, the costs of extending a scheme to include roads, areas and times of day where efficient charges are low might be very small, but with other technologies the cost of extending charging zones would be much larger. We would also need to take into account the realities 'on the ground' of the opportunities for traffic to divert from charged roads to less sensible routes on uncharged ones.

9 ROAD USER CHARGING IN PRACTICE

In previous chapters we have presented a vision of what might, in principle, be achieved by national road user charging, largely neglecting the crucial issues of technology, cost and acceptability to a sufficient proportion of the electorate. We now turn to a discussion of some of the issues that would have to be resolved before a national scheme became a reality.

Policy analysis

More robust predictions must be made of the appropriate levels of charge, the effects these might have on traffic levels and the revenues they might raise. This is a large-scale modelling exercise that will go to the limits of what is known about such questions as the responses of traffic to charges (the elasticities) and the values that road users place on their time. Since charging involves facing users with the costs they inflict on the environment as well as congestion costs, there will also be a need for the best possible evidence on the magnitudes of these environmental costs. Of course, these are requirements common to the economic analysis of many transport policies. The quality of the information is improving rapidly. While precision cannot be expected (and is probably not necessary), the basic information is better than in many other areas of public policy, and the imperfections of modelling need not prevent a full consideration of the policy.

Technologies and enforcement

There will have to be a thorough review of the technologies that might be appropriate, including cost and integrity. Initial capital costs, maintenance costs and administration costs are crucial because they can so easily consume any revenues or economic benefits the policy might generate. The London technology has worked well enough, but its costs would probably rule it out for use over a significantly larger, less dense geographical area.

The timescale over which the technologies could be real-istically expected to become reliably available would need to be assessed. This is likely to be a particular issue in the case of systems that rely on satellite positioning, because it will be a number of years before the risks associated with the use of military satel-lites can be eliminated by the arrival of European commercial satellites (called Galileo). So the question will arise as to whether an alternative method – perhaps something as simple as a paper permit – could be made to work as an interim solution.

Consideration will have to be given to how best to deal with the monumental administrative tasks. Even the relatively small London scheme is generating over 100,000 licence issues a day, and more than 900,000 Penalty Charge Notices were issued in the first eight months of operation. Further, the capabilities of the vehicle registration system will have to be confirmed as adequate for the requirements of any proposed implementation.

In order to design a successful enforcement regime, research will have to be carried out on the propensity to offend in relation to the probabilities of an offence being correctly detected (which will depend on the technology being appraised) and alternative levels of penalty.

Privacy and human rights

In the past, reservations have been expressed about the privacy and human rights issues that could be created by any system that records the movements of individuals or their vehicles. In the event, this issue seems not to have been a concern in the case of the London scheme, perhaps because the design requires records to be kept in rather limited circumstances and perhaps because public attitudes are changing on this matter. This demonstrates that in a relatively simple case such as the present London scheme it is feasible to choose a simple design that accommodates the general public's current sensitivities on this matter. It has yet to be demonstrated that this is also feasible on a national scale.

Equity and concessions

There will have to be a careful analysis of the effect of the proposed policies on different groups. In particular, assessment will be needed of the familiar proposition that user charging would disadvantage the low-income motorist. The answer on this point will depend a great deal on the nature of the policy in the round – in particular, the magnitude of the net revenues, and how and where they would be spent. For instance, if revenues were used to reduce fuel taxes and vehicle ownership taxes, it might turn out to be of benefit to the substantial number of lower-income private car users to be found in rural areas who have no realistic public transport alternative – and it might therefore make a valuable contribution to avoidance of the 'social exclusion' of sections of the rural population.

In urban areas the relationships between gainers, losers and income will depend crucially on where different income groups live in relation to the charging areas. This is likely to vary from place to place (see Santos and Newbery, 2002, and other work by these authors). It may be the case that pensioners are able to vary the time of day at which they drive and thus reduce their charges more easily.

Similarly, there are the issues relating to the likely impact on business and commerce, and the impact on freight service providers relative to private vehicles and buses. Should commercial vehicles pay more than private vehicles (because they use more road space and cause more environmental damage) or should they pay less (because they are the prime users of roads and serve industry)?

Linked to the question of incidence on particular groups is the thorny question of what discounts and concessions should be granted. There will always be immense pressure from interest groups arguing that they have a special case for exemption, and it is tempting to accede to some of them in order to gain support. The basic principle, however, is that all road users are causing some environmental damage and consuming valuable road space (including buses, taxis and commercial vehicles) and they should pay for it. Any need to compensate particular groups for social or political reasons can and should be dealt with in ways other than by granting exemptions. Too many exemptions will fatally blunt the effectiveness of the policy in reducing environmental damage and congestion, and will dilute the revenues without greatly reducing the administration costs. It is almost impossible to rescind a concession once granted.

In particular, it is not sensible to think in terms of offering major discounts to local residents unless the geographical area of their validity is extremely small. Most trips by both cars and commercial vehicles are quite short, so discounts to residents would destroy the disincentive effect of charges. Granting the 90 per cent discount to residents of the present London congestion charging scheme was a concession that the mayor, understandably, judged necessary to gain support for the first major scheme. There are not many residents in the charged area, and it does not compromise the scheme too much. It would not be possible to grant such a large discount to residents of any scheme covering a large part of London, however.

Understanding the incremental costs of capacity

While some of the benefits from road user charging derive from achieving more efficient management of the existing system, in the English context of having to deal with a rapidly growing underlying demand on a congested network, another important source of benefit comes from the reduced need to provide new road capacity. Furthermore, the newly calculated rate of charge (assuming it is correctly set) makes appraisals of decisions about whether expanding road capacity is good value for money much easier: the scheme is justified if the extra charge revenue would cover the cost of the expansion. In order to operate this simple investment rule, however, and to assess the costs avoided through moderating demand by implementing road user charging, one clearly needs to have an estimate of the costs of providing more capacity. In the UK there seems to be remarkably little information on this basic issue of how the costs of roads (and railways for that matter) vary with the capacity provided. A further advantage of a charging scheme is that it would make it possible for private companies, trusts and so on to build, maintain and manage roads, competing on an equal basis with existing road space owned and managed by various levels of government. It would also facilitate the privatisation of parts of the road network, although this, of course, leads to a number of wider issues that are not dealt with in this paper.

Land use planning and urban densities

In principle, correctly set road user charges could internalise most external effects. It is clear, however, that in practice there will always be important considerations that must be dealt with in other ways. One of the most significant of these is land use policy. It is hard to imagine that the desire to manipulate residential densities, to reduce the development of out-of-town shopping centres and so forth, could all be acceptably dealt with by means of practical road user charging. So there is an issue as to the extent to which land use policies should be moderated if road user charging were introduced.

By the same token it would be useful to be able to make more definitive predictions than seems to be possible at the moment regarding the long-term impact that charging would have on the densities and economic vitality of cities.

The effect on rail finances

The introduction of road user charging would have a major impact on the delicate issue of railway finances. It would undermine one of the main arguments deployed in defence of public subsidies, namely that they assist modal transfer from road to rail and thereby relieve road congestion. Road user charging attacks the problem directly and renders public transport subsidy unnecessary on these grounds.

In fact, it is hard to see that the distribution of public subsidy to the passenger train operating companies in the UK is closely related to modal transfer in congested road areas. For instance, the annual report of the Strategic Rail Authority shows low rates of subsidy per passenger kilometre to passenger train operating companies in the London area and much higher rates for more rural areas. But that points to another problem: railway finances in the UK tend to be strong in their major commuter markets (mainly in London) because that is where passenger densities are high, a circumstance that favours the economics of railways. These are also the situations in which there tends to be a severe shortage of rail capacity: it would be difficult to carry more rail passengers than at present. These are the same circumstances in which road user charging would strengthen the competitive position of rail and lead to more passengers, if only there were the capacity to take them. Conversely, in rural areas where rail finances are already weak and there is unused capacity, any road user charging policy that reduced the cost of motoring in rural areas would further reduce rail traffic and weaken rail finances. Put another way, road user charging would strengthen the case for more rail capacity investment in the urban areas, particularly for the

London commuter railway. There is a similar set of implications for policies towards bus and tram systems.

These are not arguments against introducing road user charging – to deploy them in that way would be to replicate the protectionist arguments that so distorted transport development in the 1920s and 1930s in the forlorn attempt to protect railways and tramways against the growing competition from road-based services. But it is necessary to recognise and respond to the budgetary and policy implications for public transport.

Revenue neutrality

It is tempting to promise that a new system of road charges would be 'revenue-neutral', meaning that taxes such as fuel duty and vehicle ownership levies would be adjusted in such a way that, say, the total of taxes and charges would be unaltered. In fact, the UK government has already made just such a commitment in relation to its firm intention to introduce distance-based taxation for commercial vehicles – though the prospective date for introducing it now seems to be slipping well beyond 2006 or 2007. The obvious attraction is that it may help to deflect opposition from the representatives of road users on the grounds that as a group they would not be paying any more taxation.

A policy of revenue neutrality at the national level creates difficulties, however. Whilst it may be neutral for the group of road users as a whole it will not be neutral from the perspective of most individuals. Those in busy, congested circumstances would be likely to pay more and those in rural areas, or who use roads at off-peak times, would pay less. Broadly, substantial amounts of money would be shifted away from the conurbations and into the rural areas. Further, if all the charge revenue were consumed by compensatory tax changes then there would be none available to pay for 'complementary measures' such as road or public transport improvements local to the charged areas. That would make it difficult to present the policy to the general public. Note that the London scheme was not revenue-neutral so far as the motorist was concerned, although it *was* neutral in the weaker sense that the legislation requires that the net revenues be spent on transport purposes in the London area.

No doubt the Treasury would, at the very least, want any scheme to provide sufficient net revenue to pay for additional public transport costs. It might go further and look for a contribution towards the present spiralling costs of both buses and railways. Roads have become a buoyant and fruitful source of general tax revenues.

Whatever policy is adopted on revenue neutrality at the national level it seems likely that road user charging will create pressure for an adjustment to the flows of cash caused by the present local government finance regime in order to mitigate the opposition from communities that would otherwise lose out. And that will take the road user charging debate into much murkier and less tractable territory.

European issues

It would seem to be essential to avoid a multiplicity of incompatible local charging systems across the UK. Arguably the same thing applies across Europe in view of the increasing volume of inter-state travel by private and commercial vehicles alike. The European Commission issued a draft Directive on Road Charging Interoperability in May 2003 which completed its first reading in the European Parliament in December. The principal aim is to further the effectiveness of the Trans-European Network and to ensure the creation of a European Electronic Toll Service that will enable technical interoperability.

Securing agreement on common technical standards across Europe will be difficult. But it would be harder still to secure agreement on common rates of charge and corresponding rates of taxation. Fuel tax rates vary considerably and attempts at tax harmonisation have been notably unsuccessful in the past. The UK carries higher rates of fuel tax than the European average. England is, however, on average, more congested than the rest of Europe, so it could be appropriate for average road user charges to be higher in England. Rather as with UK local government finance, this is a much less tractable set of issues than mere domestic transport policy.

This raises a wider set of issues still. The roads, arguably, are a utility like the electricity, gas and telecommunications networks. As those industries were privatised and economic regulation was developed, important questions were asked about the parts of the industry that formed a natural monopoly. Efforts were made to isolate the natural monopoly element for special treatment by the regulator. Similar issues apply with the road systems and road charging technology. Is it efficient to have the same user charging technology over a wide area (for example, the EU)? If it is, is it possible to separate the ownership of the roads from the charging technology so that roads owned by the governments of different countries or different private bodies and trusts can have access to the same charging technology and infrastructure? Thus there is a whole set of issues relating to the ownership and regulation of different parts of the road infrastructure and charging technology

that needs to be considered. This leads on to issues of governance.

Governance

Road users are already paying substantial charges for the use of
the system. Motorists are well aware that tax on the fuel they
buy is heavy but many are only dimly aware that it constitutes
well over 70 per cent of the price, and it is rare for them to
think of this as a charge. They would take greater interest if the
tax disc and a proportion of fuel duty were to be replaced by
an explicit distance-based charge, however. They would ask new
questions about the level of service they were getting in return
for their money. In particular, they would want to know who
would set the charges and by what objective criteria, who was
accountable for the money collected and for decisions on how
that money would be spent. Fuel tax revenue in England alone is
more than £20 billion per annum. With sums of this magnitude
involved the public would rightly insist on being satisfied that
any adjustment to the present systems met standards of prudent
and efficient administration, accountability and transparency
that, at the very least, matched the current arrangements.

In the case of the London scheme this issue was explicitly dealt
with by making the new mayor accountable and by making it a legal
requirement that all charging revenues be spent on local transport.
Similar charging powers were given to other UK local authorities
under the Transport Act 2000. Some have shown interest but so
far none has adopted them (except for a very small scheme to deal
with a special problem in Durham). One of the inhibiting factors
has been a concern that if a community adopts a local road user

charging scheme its neighbours might not and that would damage the community's competitive position. Also, as we have shown, some of the nation's congestion problems occur on long-distance motorways and strategic roads that do not naturally fall within the jurisdiction of any local authority. These are some of the reasons for considering a national scheme of road user charging. But a new national scheme would require some kind of national body to be accountable. Motorists just about tolerate the current situation whereby a central exchequer collects the money and government uses it to fund general expenditures. They might not be so tolerant under a replacement system of road user charges.

Arguably, no system buried within central government (as at present) would be accepted. The motorists' lobby will never forget the experience of the Roads Board of 1909. This was created as an earmarked fund to deal with the newly created taxes on vehicles and fuel. (The annual tax disc is still referred to as the road fund licence.) But it was raided in 1915 by the government in need of funds to pay for the war. In the words of William Rees Jeffries, 'if the motoring community placed confidence in the parliamentary undertaking that the added taxation would be spent on securing new and improved roads, they were bitterly disappointed'.

The concept of a new, independent body operating under clearly defined rules and objectives could be attractive. One candidate might be the not-for-dividend company limited by guarantee, exemplified by the newly created Network Rail. Unfortunately, in that case, the inadequacies of this particular arrangement for dealing with large public infrastructure systems are becoming visible. While the company limited by guarantee has a long and honourable history it is unlikely that it can bear the load presented by such a large, complicated and politically charged industry as the national roads system. The tried and tested concept of a public trust has much more to offer. It has a long and successful history in the ownership and administration of roads and other transport infrastructure in the UK and in North America.

Inevitably this issue becomes entangled in the debate on the current powers, or lack of them, enjoyed by local authorities, and the devolution debate. The arguments for a single national charging scheme include compatibility of technical standards, consistency in charging policies, avoidance of inter-city gaming, and proper coverage of roads (such as inter-city motorways and major roads) that are not the natural concern of any one local authority. On the other hand, transport problems are mainly local and are arguably best left to local authorities to deal with. Further, the potential scale of the administrative operation that might be implied by a national scheme is alarming – and it is yet to be established that there would be sufficient scale economies from operating fewer rather than many administrative operations.

10 A DREAM OR PRACTICAL POLICY?

In this study we have explored the potential effects of road user charging in England. We have examined a range of policy scenarios including revenue-raising and revenue-neutral charging options and economically efficient pricing. For each scenario our results have identified effects on traffic volumes, prices and fares, subsidies, environmental costs, benefits to consumers, revenue to the Exchequer, and overall net benefits.

We have shown that appropriate charging structures coupled with compensating reductions in motoring taxes could make a real difference to traffic growth, congestion and environmental damage. They could relieve the pressure to build new roads. The case for introducing charges can only become stronger as time passes.

It makes good economic sense to shift the burden of taxes and charges away from fixed taxes such as the tax disc (a tax on owner-ship), towards charges that vary with usage. Whether a govern-ment following these principles makes offsetting adjustments to fuel duty and other taxes would be a matter of policy – we have presented some reference packages that keep the total revenue from charges and taxes at roughly today's levels. These illustrate how our current system of fuel duty is a blunt instrument that fails to distinguish those circumstances in which there is a case for reducing traffic, by requiring motorists to pay the full cost of their journeys, from those in which people and industry could enjoy the benefits of greater mobility at lower cost.

Congestion and environmental charges on top of today's fuel taxes

If today's rate of fuel duty were accepted as a foundation to which environmental and congestion charges were to be added then, assuming today's traffic levels and low-end environmental costs, there would be an overall increase in the Exchequer income of about £10 billion per annum. In some, congested, places the charges would be high and the reduction in traffic would be substantial. But in many places and at many times there is little congestion, so the increase in charges would be only the relatively small environmental charge. The net result would be a reduction of 9 per cent in overall traffic levels – indicating the extent to which congestion is a localised problem. This policy could be combined with abolition of the annual tax disc.

Using high-end estimates of the environmental costs of motoring, and basing charges on requiring motorists to meet those costs, leads to an overall fall in traffic by 19 per cent. The net gain to the Exchequer rises to £15 billion per annum, and the saving in environmental costs increases from about £1 billion per annum to £5 billion per annum.

A revenue-neutral scenario

Rather than increasing the total tax take a government might decide to concentrate on improving the *balance* of charges, keeping the total constant. Revenue-neutral packages achieve a redistribution of traffic away from congested times and places and away from circumstances where environmental damage is greatest, whilst accommodating a slight increase in overall traffic. Traffic is reduced most in the big conurbations, and it increases most in the country areas. The big cities enjoy a substantial speed improvement. Many of the places that have the biggest traffic volume increase (such as rural North of England) experience little or no speed reduction – because they are areas with spare capacity and therefore relatively little congestion. This illustrates the proposition that, at today's overall rates of fuel tax, city areas are undercharged, while the country areas are significantly overcharged.

The pressure to provide more road capacity would be significantly reduced because charging moderates traffic growth in just those places where capacity is exhausted.

Economically efficient user charges

Alternatively, suppose that we were able to rebuild our system of transport charges from scratch, using first principles: abolish the present fuel duty and vehicle excise duty, minimise subsidies to public transport and calculate appropriate charges for congestion and the other costs. If low environmental damage costs are used, then compared with today's levels overall Exchequer revenues are reduced by £3.8 billion per annum. Traffic increases by 12 per cent: that for private cars by 6 per cent and that for commercial vehicles by 16 per cent. Subsidies to the bus and rail industries both fall. Overall, there is a benefit to passengers and freight of £6.8 billion per annum, although there is an environmental damage cost of £0.4 billion per annum. Average money costs per car kilometre fall from 10.4 pence to 9.3 pence. There would be a net increase in economic efficiency.

Assuming high environmental costs there would be a net gain to the Exchequer of £4.6 billion, reflecting the more aggressive stance towards charging for environmental costs: there is an estimated environmental gain of £1.6 billion per annum against the current base. Average money costs per car kilometre would rise from 10.4 pence to 11 pence.

So, if they were introduced today, the proper set of road user charges might involve road users paying more or less than currently – or approximately the same if a mid-range environmental charge were adopted. The precise outcome would depend on a number of factors, including the valuation of the environment and people's response to charging. But by 2010, increases in traffic and congestion would probably mean that, according to this set of principles, road users should pay more. What is unambiguous from our analysis is that, leaving aside the issue of the overall level of charges, there would be benefits from changes to the structure of charges road users face.

If a large change in the total revenues were judged undesirable one could preserve the idealised tax and charge *structure* but impose a mark-up or mark-down so that the direct effect on Exchequer finances is neutral. For the low environmental costs this gives the best overall net benefit of all the scenarios we considered, at £2.9 billion per annum. There is a marked improvement in bus and rail finances (partly due to the fares increases: 20 per cent and 80 per cent). There is a reduction in environmental damage valued at £0.3 billion per annum. Under the assumption of high environmental costs there is a net gain to the Exchequer of £2.3 billion per annum, a reduction in environmental damage costs of £0.8 billion per annum and an overall economic benefit of £3.8 billion per annum. Of course, there is less of a tendency to reduce charges in non-urban areas than under the low environmental cost case.

Thus, in considering the practicalities of introducing road user charging, it can be said that, whilst any scheme of charging would lead to redistribution of taxes and charges between different groups of motorists, there are various ways in which a policy can be developed that is approximately revenue-neutral.

How extensive should charging be?

Depending on the costs of the technology chosen to implement road user charging, it may be too troublesome to levy the smaller rates of charge or to attempt to cover all areas, except through a component of conventional fuel duty. We have offered indicative estimates of what the effect might be of waiving low charges or restricting geographical coverage.

Using the low environmental costs and the scenario where user charges are added to the present fuel taxes, we found that raising the threshold below which no user charges were imposed on vehicles makes little difference between a threshold of about 5 pence per car kilometre and one of about 16 pence per car kilometre. Excluding rural and small urban areas from charging would reduce the proportion of the traffic being charged from 92 to 45 per cent, but would reduce the revenues only from £11.5 to £9.2 billion per annum. Imposing a threshold below which no charges are made of 5 pence per car kilometre further reduces the revenue to £5.3 billion per annum, but this means that only about 10 per cent of the traffic is experiencing any charge at all, apart from fuel duty. This would achieve a 2 per cent reduction in national traffic, but a much higher proportionate reduction in those congested circumstances to which the charges would apply.

If London, the conurbations and big urban areas only were included, and if the threshold of 5 pence per car kilometre were to apply, the revenue would be over £4 billion per annum, but only 8 per cent of national traffic would experience charging.

There are clearly serious practical issues for politicians to consider here. The marginal costs of extending the area over which charges are levied and extending the times of day at which charging takes place may be relatively small with some charging systems. The adoption of such systems would imply charging more widely. Such charging systems, perhaps involving satellite technology, might also bring other benefits and have other economic uses. Other charging systems, such as paper-based and zonal-based charging systems, may cost more to extend to areas and times of day when charges would be low. There are no issues of principle here. But there is a question to be addressed as to how a scheme should be implemented in practice.

Location-based services: the wider vision

This study concentrates on the vision of what national road user charging could offer for 'conventional' transport policy. This vision goes much further, however, because equipment installed for that purpose may have other applications – generically called location-based services. Some of these already exist in some form. For instance, it might offer:

- in-vehicle navigation;
- real-time best-route guidance;

- facilities to aid authorities in managing the road network;
- the opportunity for commercial vehicle and bus managers to track vehicles;
- the opportunity to track stolen vehicles.

Insurance markets would be revolutionised by the ability to achieve a closer match between insurance premiums and usage-based risk. If the equipment could achieve both adequate accuracy and adequate integrity then it could be used for various enforcement tasks, such as:

- speed limits;
- drivers' hours regulations;
- parking offences.

The potential for cheaper and more effective law enforcement is huge.

Public transport operators are already beginning to introduce electronic ticketing, for example the London Oyster card, which stores value and engages in wireless communication between the card and London Transport's equipment. In principle these devices might also be used as a basis for road user charging, thus offering truly integrated transport charging. They already offer the potential for shifting public subsidies away from the present operator-based subsidies towards much more accurately targeted, and hence more policy-effective, direct subsidies to users.

Finally, it is certain that once such a system became established the retail and financial services industries would find ways of offering value-added services such as electronic cash, credit and communications.

A dream or practical policy?

Road user charging to reflect congestion and environmental damage offers a new dimension to transport policy. This has been recognised by politicians and the general public after its practical demonstration in London. Serious consideration is now being given to extending the idea on a national level.

We have shown that the policy has a great deal to offer. Indeed, we think that there is no real alternative to a more constructive use of price as a way of managing a steadily worsening problem. We have argued that, in combination with other location-based services, road user charging could fundamentally change the way we manage mobility, with great overall benefit.

But if this is to be achieved a number of problems must be resolved. Some of the obstacles are technological and others economic. The decongestion benefits of road user charging fall rapidly away from the most congested places. Hence it may prove impossible to justify the implementation costs at all but a few locations. Standard fuel tax is well established, cheap to collect, hard to evade and can be made to do part of the job of reflecting environmental damage. Nevertheless, there is plenty of scope for improvements to the existing set of vehicle ownership and use charges and taxes.

The most difficult problems to be resolved before road user charging could become a reality relate to governance and political economy. How would it affect the financial position of public transport? Would that matter? Who would gain and who would lose? And, in particular, who would have control of charge revenues and expenditures?

The theoretical case for road user charging is well established and the London experience has demonstrated that large-scale schemes can be practical and beneficial. How long it takes for road user charging to be seen by policy-makers as a practical proposition on a national scale remains to be seen. But until it is implemented it is hard to see how continual repetition of the past failures in transport policy can be avoided. If it can be introduced successfully then it will greatly improve the performance of one of the most important sectors of the economy.

REFERENCES

ATOC (2001), *Passenger Demand Forecasting Handbook*, London: ATOC.

Bell, B. G. H., M. A. Quddus, J.-D. Schmocker and A. Fonzone (2004), *The Impact of the Congestion Charge on the Retail Sector*, London: John Lewis Partnership, http://www.john-lewis-partnership.co.uk/downloads/BellReport.pdf.

Buchanan, C. (1963), *Traffic in Towns*, London: HMSO.

Coates, J. (1999), *Roads to Accountability*, Basingstoke: Automobile Association.

Dargay, J. and M. Hanly (1999), *Bus Fare Elasticities: Report to the Department of Environment, Transport and the Regions*, London: ESRC Transport Studies Unit, ref. 1999/26, University College.

DETR (2000a), *Transport 2010: The Ten Year Plan*, London: Department of Environment, Transport and the Regions.

DETR (2000b), *Transport Ten Year Plan 2000: Background analysis*, London: Department of Environment, Transport and the Regions.

DETR (2001), *Transport Economics Note*, London: Department of Environment, Transport and the Regions.

DfT (2002), *Transport Ten Year Plan 2000: Delivering better transport – progress report*, London: Department for Transport, December.

DfT (2003), *Managing Our Roads*, London: Department for Transport.

DTLR (2001a), *Transport Statistics, Great Britain: 2001 Edition*, London: The Stationery Office.

DTLR (2001b), *Regional Transport Statistics*, London: The Stationery Office.

Glaister, S. (2002), 'UK Transport Policy 1997–2001', *Oxford Review of Economic Policy*, 18(2): 154–86.

Glaister, S. and D. J. Graham (2003a), *Transport Pricing and Investment in England: Technical report*, working paper, London: Imperial College, http://www.cts.cv.ic. ac.uk/html/ResearchActivities/publicationDetails. asp?PublicationID=307.

Glaister, S. and D. J. Graham (2003b), *An Evaluation of Road User Charging in England*, working paper, London: Imperial College.

Government Office for London (2000), *Road Charging Options for London*, Norwich: HMSO.

Graham, D. J. and S. Glaister (2002a), 'The demand for automobile fuel: a survey of elasticities', *Journal of Transport Economics and Policy*, 36: 1–26.

Graham, D. J. and S. Glaister (2002b), *Review of Income and Price Elasticities of Demand for Road Traffic*, report to the Department for Transport, London.

Graham, D. J. and S. Glaister (2003), *Spatial Implications of Transport Pricing*, working paper, London: Imperial College.

Graham, D. J. and S. Glaister (2004), 'A review of road traffic demand elasticity estimates', *Transport Reviews*, 24(3).

Grayling, T. and S. Glaister (2000), *A New Fares Contract for London*, London: IPPR.

Greater London Council (1974), *Study of Supplementary Licensing*, London: GLC.

Hibbs, J. (1993), *Market for Mobility*, Hobart Paper 121, London: Institute for Economic Affairs.

Hibbs, J. and G. Roth (1992), *Tomorrow's Way: Managing Roads in a Free Society*, London: Adam Smith Institute.

House of Commons Transport Committee (2003), *Jam Tomorrow?: The Multi Modal Study Investment Plans*, London: HC38, April.

Newbery, D. (2002), *Road User and Congestion Charges*, mimeo, University of Cambridge, August.

Roth, G. (1995), *Roads in a Market Economy*, Aldershot: Avebury.

Sansom, T., C. A. Nash, P. J. Mackie and J. Shires (2001), *Surface Transport Costs and Charges: Final report for the Department of Transport, Environment and the Regions*, Institute for Transport Studies, University of Leeds, April.

Santos, G. and D. M. Newbery (2002), *Estimating Urban Road Congestion Charges*, CEPR Discussion Paper 3176, University of Cambridge.

Smeed, R. (1964), *Road Pricing: The Economic and Technical Possibilities*, London: HMSO.

SRA (2003), *Everyone's Railway: the Wider Case for Rail*, London: Strategic Rail Authority, September.

Transport for London (2003), *Congestion Charging: Six Months On*, October, www.TfL.gov.uk.

Transport for London (2004), *Congestion Charging: Update on Scheme Impacts and Operations*, February, www.TfL.gov.uk.

Walters, A. A. (1961), 'The theory and measurement of private and social costs of highway congestion', *Econometrica*, 29(4).

ABOUT THE IEA

The Institute is a research and educational charity (No. CC 235 351), limited by guarantee. Its mission is to improve understanding of the fundamental institutions of a free society with particular reference to the role of markets in solving economic and social problems.

The IEA achieves its mission by:

- a high-quality publishing programme
- conferences, seminars, lectures and other events
- outreach to school and college students
- brokering media introductions and appearances

The IEA, which was established in 1955 by the late Sir Antony Fisher, is an educational charity, not a political organisation. It is independent of any political party or group and does not carry on activities intended to affect support for any political party or candidate in any election or referendum, or at any other time. It is financed by sales of publications, conference fees and voluntary donations.

In addition to its main series of publications the IEA also publishes a quarterly journal, *Economic Affairs*.

The IEA is aided in its work by a distinguished international Academic Advisory Council and an eminent panel of Honorary Fellows. Together with other academics, they review prospective IEA publications, their comments being passed on anonymously to authors. All IEA papers are therefore subject to the same rigorous independent refereeing process as used by leading academic journals.

IEA publications enjoy widespread classroom use and course adoptions in schools and universities. They are also sold throughout the world and often translated/reprinted.

Since 1974 the IEA has helped to create a world-wide network of 100 similar institutions in over 70 countries. They are all independent but share the IEA's mission.

Views expressed in the IEA's publications are those of the authors, not those of the Institute (which has no corporate view), its Managing Trustees, Academic Advisory Council members or senior staff.

Members of the Institute's Academic Advisory Council, Honorary Fellows, Trustees and Staff are listed on the following page.

The Institute gratefully acknowledges financial support for its publications programme and other work from a generous benefaction by the late Alec and Beryl Warren.

131

Other papers recently published by the IEA include:

WHO, What and Why?

Transnational Government, Legitimacy and the World Health Organization
Roger Scruton
Occasional Paper 113; ISBN 0 255 36487 3
£8.00

The World Turned Rightside Up

A New Trading Agenda for the Age of Globalisation
John C. Hulsman
Occasional Paper 114; ISBN 0 255 36495 4
£8.00

The Representation of Business in English Literature

Introduced and edited by Arthur Pollard
Readings 53; ISBN 0 255 36491 1
£12.00

Anti-Liberalism 2000

The Rise of New Millennium Collectivism
David Henderson
Occasional Paper 115; ISBN 0 255 36497 0
£7.50

Capitalism, Morality and Markets

Brian Griffiths, Robert A. Sirico, Norman Barry & Frank Field
Readings 54; ISBN 0 255 36496 2
£7.50

A Conversation with Harris and Seldon

Ralph Harris & Arthur Seldon
Occasional Paper 116; ISBN 0 255 36498 9
£7.50

Malaria and the DDT Story

Richard Tren & Roger Bate
Occasional Paper 117; ISBN 0 255 36499 7
£10.00

A Plea to Economists Who Favour Liberty: Assist the Everyman

Daniel B. Klein
Occasional Paper 118; ISBN 0 255 36501 2
£10.00

The Changing Fortunes of Economic Liberalism

Yesterday, Today and Tomorrow
David Henderson
Occasional Paper 105 (new edition); ISBN 0 255 36520 9
£12.50

The Global Education Industry

Lessons from Private Education in Developing Countries

James Tooley

Hobart Paper 141 (new edition); ISBN 0 255 36503 9

£12.50

Saving Our Streams

The Role of the Anglers' Conservation Association in Protecting English and Welsh Rivers

Roger Bate

Research Monograph 53; ISBN 0 255 36494 6

£10.00

Better Off Out?

The Benefits or Costs of EU Membership

Brian Hindley & Martin Howe

Occasional Paper 99 (new edition); ISBN 0 255 36502 0

£10.00

Buckingham at 25

Freeing the Universities from State Control

Edited by James Tooley

Readings 55; ISBN 0 255 36512 8

£15.00

Lectures on Regulatory and Competition Policy
Irwin M. Stelzer
Occasional Paper 120; ISBN 0 255 36511 X
£12.50

Misguided Virtue
False Notions of Corporate Social Responsibility
David Henderson
Hobart Paper 142; ISBN 0 255 36510 1
£12.50

HIV and Aids in Schools
The Political Economy of Pressure Groups and Miseducation
Barrie Craven, Pauline Dixon, Gordon Stewart & James Tooley
Occasional Paper 121; ISBN 0 255 36522 5
£10.00

The Road to Serfdom
The Reader's Digest *condensed version*
Friedrich A. Hayek
Occasional Paper 122; ISBN 0 255 36530 6
£7.50

Bastiat's *The Law*

Introduction by Norman Barry

Occasional Paper 123; ISBN 0 255 36509 8

£7.50

A Globalist Manifesto for Public Policy

Charles Calomiris

Occasional Paper 124; ISBN 0 255 36525 X

£7.50

Euthanasia for Death Duties

Putting Inheritance Tax Out of Its Misery

Barry Bracewell-Milnes

Research Monograph 54; ISBN 0 255 36513 6

£10.00

Liberating the Land

The Case for Private Land-use Planning

Mark Pennington

Hobart Paper 143; ISBN 0 255 36508 X

£10.00

Capital Controls: a 'Cure' Worse Than the Problem?

Forrest Capie

Research Monograph 56; ISBN 0 255 36506 3

£10.00

The Poverty of 'Development Economics'

Deepak Lal

Hobart Paper 144 (reissue); ISBN 0 255 36519 5

£15.00

Should Britain Join the Euro?

The Chancellor's Five Tests Examined

Patrick Minford

Occasional Paper 126; ISBN 0 255 36527 6

£7.50

Post-Communist Transition: Some Lessons

Leszek Balcerowicz

Occasional Paper 127; ISBN 0 255 36533 0

£7.50

A Tribute to Peter Bauer

John Blundell et al.

Occasional Paper 128; ISBN 0 255 36531 4

£10.00

Employment Tribunals

Their Growth and the Case for Radical Reform
J. R. Shackleton
Hobart Paper 145; ISBN 0 255 36515 2
£10.00

Fifty Economic Fallacies Exposed

Geoffrey E. Wood
Occasional Paper 129; ISBN 0 255 36518 7
£12.50

A Market in Airport Slots

Keith Boyfield (editor), David Starkie, Tom Bass & Barry Humphreys
Readings 56; ISBN 0 255 36505 5
£10.00

Money, Inflation and the Constitutional Position of the Central Bank

Milton Friedman & Charles A. E. Goodhart
Readings 57; ISBN 0 255 36538 1
£10.00

railway.com
Parallels between the early British railways and the ICT revolution
Robert C. B. Miller
Research Monograph 57; ISBN 0 255 36534 9
£12.50

The Regulation of Financial Markets
Edited by Philip Booth & David Currie
Readings 58; ISBN 0 255 36551 9
£12.50

Climate Alarmism Reconsidered
Robert L. Bradley Jr
Hobart Paper 146; ISBN 0 255 36541 1
£12.50

Government Failure: E. G. West on Education
Edited by James Tooley & James Stanfield
Occasional Paper 130; ISBN 0 255 36552 7
£12.50

Waging the War of Ideas
John Blundell
Second edition
Occasional Paper 131; ISBN 0 255 36547 0
£12.50

Corporate Governance: Accountability in the Marketplace
Elaine Sternberg
Second edition
Hobart Paper 147; ISBN 0 255 36542 X
£12.50

The Land Use Planning System
Evaluating Options for Reform
John Corkindale
Hobart Paper 148; ISBN 0 255 36550 0
£10.00

Economy and Virtue
Essays on the Theme of Markets and Morality
Edited by Dennis O'Keeffe
Readings 59; ISBN 0 255 36504 7
£12.50

Free Markets Under Siege
Cartels, Politics and Social Welfare
Richard A. Epstein
Occasional Paper 132; ISBN 0 255 36553 5
£10.00

Unshackling Accountants
D. R. Myddelton
Hobart Paper 149; ISBN 0 255 36559 4
£12.50

The Euro as Politics
Pedro Schwartz
Research Monograph 58; ISBN 0 255 36535 7
£12.50

To order copies of currently available IEA papers, or to enquire about availability, please contact:

Lavis Marketing
IEA orders
FREEPOST LON21280
Oxford OX3 7BR

Tel: 01865 767575
Fax: 01865 750079
Email: orders@lavismarketing.co.uk

The IEA also offers a subscription service to its publications. For a single annual payment, currently £40.00 in the UK, you will receive every title the IEA publishes during the course of a year, invitations to events, and discounts on our extensive back catalogue. For more information, please contact:

Subscriptions
The Institute of Economic Affairs
2 Lord North Street
London SW1P 3LB

Tel: 020 7799 8900
Fax: 020 7799 2137
Website: www.iea.org.uk